Exploring Faith Questions

Journeys of Spirituality and Discovery

by Anne Martin

UNITED CHURCH
PUBLISHING HOUSE
Toronto, Canada

Exploring Faith Questions: Journeys of Spirituality and Discovery

Library and Archives Canada Cataloguing in Publication

Martin, Anne (Anne Marie), 1951-
Exploring faith questions : journeys of spirituality and discovery / by Anne Martin.

Includes bibliographical references.
ISBN 1-55134-135-2

1. Spiritual life--Christianity. 2. Devotional exercises. I. Title.

BV4511.M37 2004 248.4 C2004-903099-X

United Church Publishing House
3250 Bloor St. West, Suite 300
Toronto, ON
Canada M8X 2Y4
416-231-5931
bookpub@united-church.ca
www.united-church.ca/upch

Design and Production: Graphics and Print
Cover Photo © Claudia Kutchukian

Printed in Canada

5 4 3 2 08 07 06 05

040384

Table of Contents

A New Creed

We are not alone,
we live in God's world.

We believe in God:
who has created and is creating,
who has come in Jesus,
the Word made flesh,
to reconcile and make new,
who works in us and others
by the Spirit.

We trust in God.

We are called to be the Church:
to celebrate God's presence,
to live with respect in Creation,
to love and serve others,
to seek justice and resist evil,
to proclaim Jesus, crucified and risen,
our judge and our hope.

In life, in death, in life beyond death,
God is with us.

We are not alone.

Thanks be to God.

Adopted by the 23rd General Council of The United Church of Canada, 1968

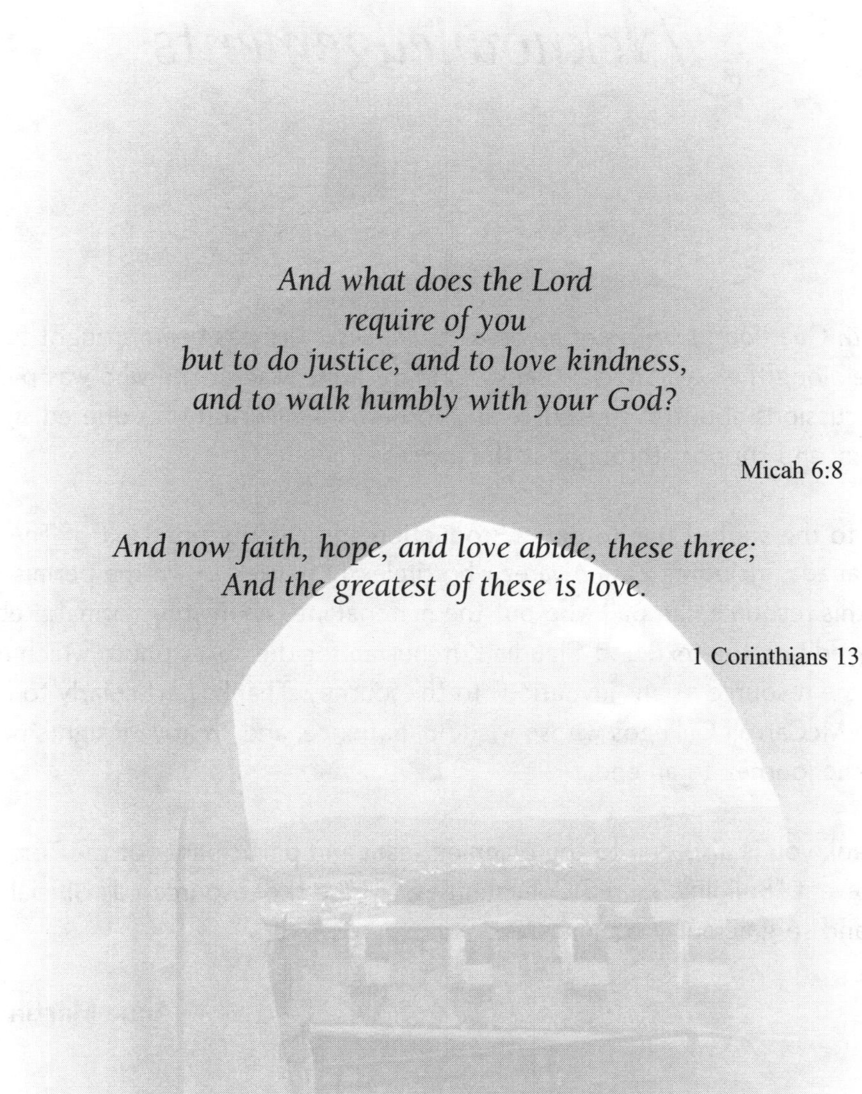

And what does the Lord
require of you
but to do justice, and to love kindness,
and to walk humbly with your God?

Micah 6:8

And now faith, hope, and love abide, these three;
And the greatest of these is love.

1 Corinthians 13:13

Acknowledgements

Exploring Faith Questions: Journeys of Spirituality and Discovery has been brought to life by many people along the way. Special thanks to Mary Anne MacFarlane who was part of the very first discussions about this resource and to Barbara Fullerton who offered significant input, wisdom, and support throughout the process.

Thanks also to the staff of the Resource Production and Distribution Unit of The United Church of Canada, including Zara Alvarez who tirelessly tracked down the permissions needed for this resource, Ian Ball who put the material into an inviting format, Rebekah Chevalier for editing the text, and Claudia Kutchukian for the cover photo which is also used throughout the resource as an "invitation" to the journey. Thanks particularly to Managing Editor Aaron McCarroll Gallegos whose wisdom, patience, and creative insights helped bring this part of the journey to an end.

A special thank you is also due to the planning team and participants of the Toronto Conference event "Building Sacred Communities," where the resource was officially introduced and so graciously commended.

—Anne Martin

Introduction

Exploring Faith Questions: Journeys of Spirituality and Discovery

Welcome to *Exploring Faith Questions: Journeys of Spirituality and Discovery*. Journeys are a central theme of the Christian community. There are many journey stories to tell. We only need to think of the Israelites who journeyed from Egypt into the desert and across the River Jordan; of Ruth and Naomi who left Moab for the land of Judah; of the women and men who accompanied Jesus throughout Palestine; of the people who spread the news of Jesus throughout the Roman Empire; of the women and men who journeyed throughout the centuries in their response to God's call.

But what does it mean to explore faith questions? What can you expect as you set out with others on this journey of exploration? What if you feel that your faith is on rocky ground or you question whether you have any faith at all? What about others who seem to be sure of their faith and have a deep sense of their spirituality and connection to God? Is this exploration really for you?

What is being asked of you? You are invited to take part in an exploration, a journey of discovery. This is neither a guided tour where the leader knows everything and wants to show you the way, moving you along to keep up with the rest of the crowd. Nor is this a leisurely cruise where you are expected just to sit back and be pampered, without any demands being placed on you. This is an invitation to take part in an adventure, beginning with your own personal experience and that of the women and men who accompany you. You won't be asked to go very far in kilometres, only to your church or another participant's house. However, you will be encouraged to journey deep within yourself as you explore central faith questions.

There are no prerequisites for this exploration and no need to be at a particular place in your own personal journey. You are simply asked to be part of a small group, be willing to participate as fully as possible, and be willing to allow others to do the same. To help you on your journey, during each meeting, try to spend time doing some form of prayer or spiritual exercise with the other participants. It helps to understand that the spiritual journey is not merely an intellectual exercise but very much one of the heart and soul. Although some participants feel uncomfortable with prayer or find it burdensome, the importance of prayer for the spiritual journey cannot be stressed enough. It is through prayer that we connect with God and learn to open ourselves to God. It is also through prayer that we come into community with others more fully.

We recognize the importance of prayer by experiencing it. The experience of prayer is truly an experience to take part in and to learn from, something to nurture and savour, individually and as a group. As you explore the different themes together after praying together, you will find that, as an individual and as a group, your exploration will become richer as you become more deeply grounded in your experience of God.

Exploring Faith Questions: Journeys of Spirituality and Discovery is an invitation to explore and grow with others as you explore questions to:

- become more aware of your own personal faith journey;
- deepen your personal faith and relationship with God;
- find support for your faith journey;
- support the faith journeys of others;
- consider ways in which your faith challenges you to act more compassionately and justly within the world.

We invite you to join us.

Blessings on your journey.

Using This Workbook

This workbook is designed to give you space and inspiration to explore your faith questions. First, begin with your own experience. A few exercises included for each question will help you begin with where you are on your personal faith journey.

Personal Exploration

Before each meeting, take time to do some personal work. There is space provided for you to explore each faith question.

Process for Personal Work

Take your time: set aside about half an hour to an hour of uninterrupted time for each question.

Create "sacred space": find a quiet and comfortable space for this exercise. Perhaps light a candle.

Pray: spend a few minutes in prayer to centre yourself and ask God to help you to be open to God's presence.

Respond: let words or images come to mind, whether positive or challenging, whether or not they make sense. Write these around the theme word or phrase.

Reflect: explore the feelings attached to these words or images and some of your experiences associated with them. Which feelings are the strongest and elicit the deepest emotions? Which experiences are powerful, disturbing, enriching, or perhaps life-changing?

After you have completed this part of the exercise, turn to the following page of each chapter and write your responses to the following questions:

How has your understanding of the faith question changed over the years?

How have these changes affected the way you live in the world, that is, your understanding of holistic stewardship*?

Biblical Texts and Quotations

Biblical Texts

Biblical passages, selected to help you explore more deeply your own biblical understanding of the theme and lead to group discussion, are included for each faith question. These are *not* examples of scriptural authority on the question that you are expected to agree with. Nor do they reflect a theological understanding of the theme that you are expected to embrace. You may find some of the passages "difficult" or "challenging." If this is the case, feel free to discuss your concerns with the rest of the group.

Other Quotes

Non-biblical quotes are also included for each faith question, accompanied by the author's surname, the year of publication of the source, and the page number(s). All sources are found in the References section. You are not expected to agree with these quotes; they have been selected to help you explore further your understanding of the theme and open up discussion by presenting reflections on the theme to encourage conversation.

Members of your group may wish to take turns reading the quotes out loud, pausing after each one to note any thoughts or emotions. Does the quote inspire, surprise, anger, confuse,

* Holistic **stewardship** or discipleship is the way that we live out who we are in God's world. In response to the "giftedness" we feel in relationship to God through prayer and spiritual discipline, we are moved to take faithful action "in God's name" in our world. This means that the decisions we take, the actions we employ, and the resources we use to support those actions, are all motivated by our need to respond to God's ongoing presence and activity in our lives and our world. This is stewardship and it is fundamental to who we are as a people of faith.

console, amuse, or leave you cold? What issues, questions, or concerns does the quote raise? How does the quote relate to your own personal experiences?

Please note that you are encouraged to read the biblical passages and quotes *after* you have completed your initial reflection of the theme so that you can start exploring the theme using your own experiences rather than responding or reacting to outside material.

Suggested Group Questions

For each faith question a few questions have been provided for group discussion. Members of your group may decide to use them to help deepen your discussion.

Space for Notes

You may write your personal notes in the page provided for each question. You may also wish to do some journaling between meetings.

Selected Reading for Further Exploration

You will also find a list of books related to the faith question you have been exploring. Some of the books are applicable under a couple of question areas but have only been placed under one.

You may read some of these books on your own, or study them as part of another covenant group after you have finished the current sessions. You may wish to share other books related to the faith question.

Spiritual / Prayer Practices

This workbook contains examples of prayer practices, specially selected for group work. Groups are encouraged to use Praying with Scripture as a spiritual practice. (see Appendix B.)

About This Resource

This resource has been designed for covenant groups, small groups of three to seven participants. Each group develops a covenant outlining the participants' commitment to the group. The resource could, however, also be used for individual reflection.

Each group will decide how many meetings it wants to covenant for. It may, for example, decide to meet for eight weeks and do Questions 2-7. Once these questions are done the group may decide to meet again, this time for seven weeks, and do Questions 8-12. Since meetings 1 and 13 are introductory and final sessions respectively, each covenant period will include these in some form or another.

The material is meant to provide groups with a starting point for their time together. The group may find that it wants to spend a couple of weeks on one of the questions and save one or more of them for a later time. After completing a covenant a group may wish to focus on one of the questions, or a topic arising from it, for a few weeks, perhaps using one of the resources from the list provided.

For information on facilitating an *Exploring Faith Questions* covenant group see Appendix A.

Meeting Format *

Meal
Gathering Time
Opening
Check-in
Spiritual Practices/Prayer
Theme Exploration
Checkout
Closing

*For a discussion of the meeting format see Appendix A, page 147.

Introductory Meeting

Beginning the Journey, Considering the Questions

(*For information on facilitating an* Exploring Faith Questions *covenant group, see Appendix A.*)

Suggested Praying with Scripture passage: Luke 18:35–43

You show me the path of life. In your presence there is fullness of joy…

Psalm 16:11

Listen! I am standing at the door,
knocking; if you hear my voice and open the door,
I will come in to you and eat with you,
and you with me.

Revelation 3:20

Suggested Group Questions:

What does it mean to be part of a covenant group?
Which sessions do you wish to do together?
How do you want to approach the prayer part of the meeting?
Do you bring any concerns to the group?
What are your needs?
What are your expectations?

My Notes

Question 1

Faith: What is it? How can we talk about it?

Meeting Format

Meal

Gathering Time

Opening

Check-in

Spiritual Practices/Prayer:
Praying with Scripture: Psalm 139:1-6

Theme Exploration:
Faith

Checkout

Closing

Suggested Praying with Scripture passage: Psalm 139:1–6

O Lord, you have searched me and known me.

You know when I sit down and when I rise up; you discern my thoughts from far away.

You search out my path and my lying down, and are acquainted with all my ways.

Even before a word is on my tongue, O Lord, you know it completely.

You hem me in, behind and before, and lay your hand upon me.

Such knowledge is too wonderful for me; it is so high that I cannot attain it.

See page 155 for information on Praying with Scripture.

Personal Exploration

What words or images, whether positive or challenging, do you associate with the word below? Explore the feelings that they evoke and some of the experiences attached to them.

Faith

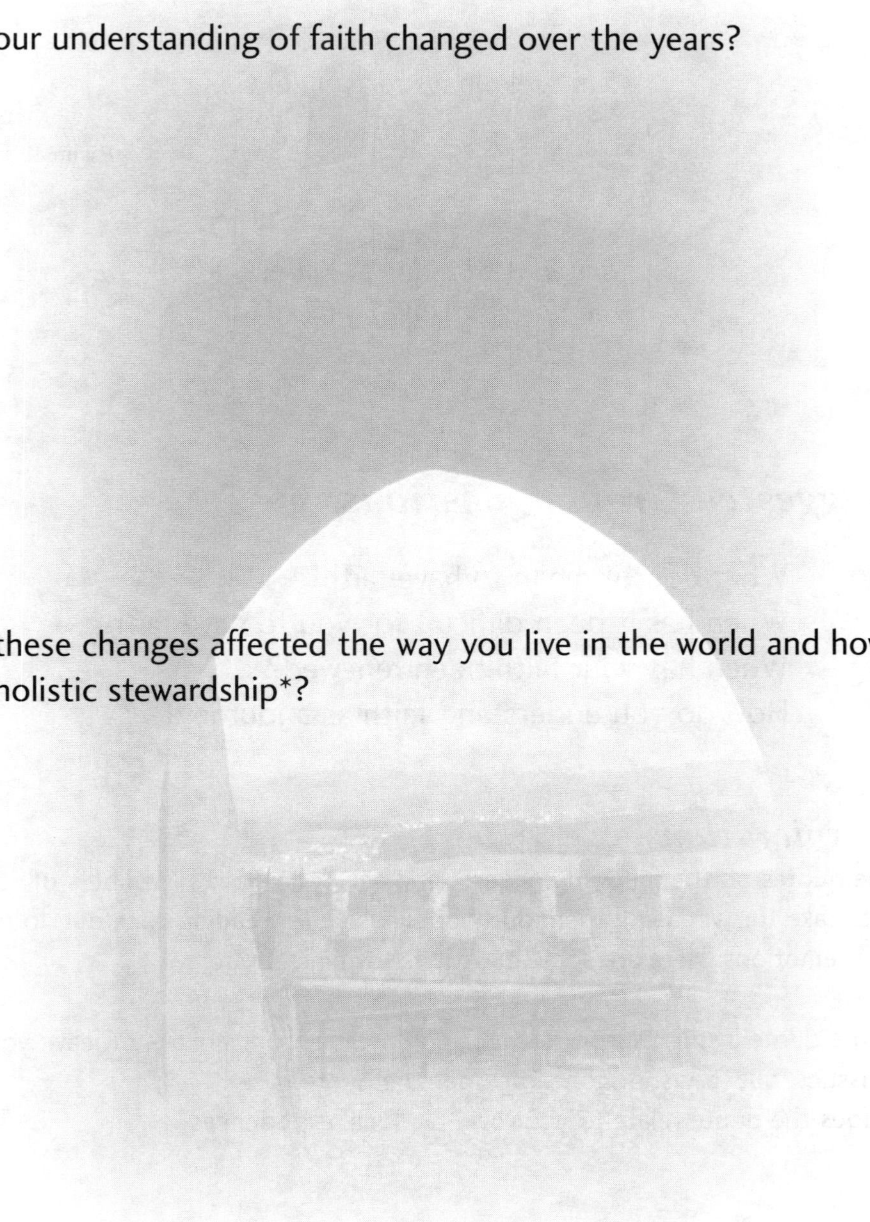

How has your understanding of faith changed over the years?

How have these changes affected the way you live in the world and how you engage in holistic stewardship*?

*See definition on page 10.

Faith: What is it? How can we talk about it?

As a deer longs for flowing streams,
so my soul longs for you, O God.

Psalm 42:1

...and he said to him, "Follow me."
And he got up and followed him.

Mark 2:14

Suggested Group Questions:

What does it mean to have faith?
When has it been difficult for you to have faith?
When has your faith been renewed?
How do you understand faith as a journey?

Group Exploration

Turn to the quotes on the following pages. Read each one slowly. Members of your group may wish to take turns reading them out loud. Pause after reading each one to note any thoughts or emotions. Here are some questions to think about:

Does the quote inspire, surprise, anger, confuse, console, amuse, or leave you cold?
What issues, questions, or concerns does the quote raise?
How does the quote relate to your own personal experiences?

Quotes

We know that there is a pilgrimage to make. It is a journey away from the self and into the mystery of God. It is an amazing grace that each of us can and does know this, or at least suspect it. To know it is really to know everything because we have only to begin and continue. To be on the pilgrimage is everything.

Main (2002: p.120)

One of my cardinal beliefs is that each of us must work earnestly to come to his or her own beliefs and then take full responsibility for them.

Harpur (1996: p.57)

A faith based solely on individual belief and disconnected from public responsibilities and actions allows the young rich rulers of our time to claim to be followers and disciples. If the words of Jesus are as true today as they were two thousand years ago, then "how hard it is for those [of the dominant culture] to enter into the reign of God. For it is easier for a camel to go through an eye of a needle than for [those of the privileged center] to enter into the reign of God" (Luke 18:24-25).

de la Torre (2002: p.141)

For us to dare to live a life in which we continue to move out of static places and take trusting steps in new directions—that is what faith is all about. The Greek word for faith means to trust—to trust that the ground before you that you have never walked on is safe ground, God's ground, holy ground.

Nouwen (2001: p.74)

(quotes continued on next page)

Quotes *(continued)*

"Faith"

Where is faith found?
not in a book,
or in a church,
not often or
for everyone.
In childish times
it's easier;
a child believes
just what it's told.
But children grow
and soon begin
to see too much
that doesn't match
the simple tales,
and not enough
of what's behind
their parents' words.
There is no God,
the cynics say;
we made him up
out of our need
and fear of death.
And happily
they offer up
their test-tube proofs.
A mystery,
the priests all say,
and point to saints
who prove their faith
in acts of love
and sacrifice.
But what of us
who are not saints,
only common
human sinners?
And what of those
who in their need
and pain cry out
to God and go
on suffering?
I do not know –
I wish I did.
Sometimes I feel
all the world's pain.
I only say
that once in my
own need I felt
a light and warm
and loving touch
that eased my soul
and banished doubt
and let me go
on to the end.
It is not proof—
there can be none.
Faith's what you find
when you're alone
and find you're not.

Anderson (1993: pp.117–118)

My Notes

Suggested Reading for Further Exploration

Anderson, Terry A., *Den of Lions: Memoirs of Seven Years* (New York: Random House, Ballantine Books, 1993).

Hutchinson, Joyce, and Joyce Rupp, *May I Walk You Home? Courage and Comfort for Caregivers of the Very Ill* (Notre Dame, IN: Ave Maria Press, 1999).

Langford, Jeremy, *God Moments: Why Faith Really Matters to a New Generation* (Maryknoll, NY: Orbis Books, 2001).

McCall Tigert, Leanne, *Coming Out Through Fire: Surviving the Trauma of Homophobia* (Cleveland, Ohio: Pilgrim Press, The United Church Press, 1999).

Myss, Caroline, *Anatomy of the Spirit: The Seven Stages of Power and Healing* (New York: Random House of Canada, Crown Publishing Group Ltd., 1996).

Weems, Renita, *Listening for God: A Minister's Journey Through Silence and Doubt* (New York: Simon & Schuster Adult Publishing Group, 2000).

Question 2

How do you experience God in your life?

Meeting Format

Meal

Gathering Time

Opening

Check-in

Spiritual Practices/Prayer:
Praying with Scripture: Acts 17:22-28

Theme Exploration:
Experiencing God

Checkout

Closing

Suggested Praying with Scripture passage: Acts 17:22-28

Then Paul stood in front of the Areopagus and said, "Athenians, I see how extremely religious you are in every way. For as I went through the city and looked carefully at the objects of your worship, I found among them an altar with the inscription, 'To an unknown god.' What therefore you worship as unknown, this I proclaim to you. The God who made the world and everything in it, ...who is Lord of heaven and earth, does not live in shrines made by human hands, nor is [God] served by human hands, as though [God] needed anything, since [God] gives to all mortals life and breath and all things. From one ancestor [God] made all nations to inhabit the whole earth, and ...allotted the times of their existence and the boundaries of the places where they would live, so that they would search for God and perhaps grope for [God] and find [God]—though indeed [God] is not far from each one of us. For 'In [God] we live and move and have our being'; as even some of your own poets have said, 'For we too are [God's] offspring.'

See page 155 for information on Praying with Scripture.

Personal Exploration

What words or images, whether positive or challenging, do you associate with the phrase below? Explore the feelings that they evoke and some of the experiences attached to them.

Experiencing God

How has your experience of God changed over the years?

How have these changes affected the way you live in the world and how you engage in holistic stewardship*?

*See definition on page 10.

How do you experience God in your life?

The kingdom of heaven is like yeast that a woman took
and mixed in with three measures of flour until all of it was leavened.

Matthew 13:33

This is the day that the Lord has made;
let us rejoice and be glad in it.

Psalm 118:24

Suggested Group Questions:

Where, when, and how have you experienced God in your life?
How has that experience changed over the years?
What is the "nature" of the God you experience?

Group Exploration

Turn to the quotes on the following pages. Read each one slowly. Members of your group may wish to take turns reading them out loud. Pause after reading each one to note any thoughts or emotions. Here are some questions to think about:

Does the quote inspire, surprise, anger, confuse, console, amuse, or leave you cold?
What issues, questions, or concerns does the quote raise?
How does the quote relate to your own personal experiences?

Quotes

What is an inadequate life? It is any life lived out of touch with nature, with the rhythm of the days, with the seasons of the year, with the softness of water, the emergence of fire, the clarity of air, the moisture of good earth. Anything else is not life. It is, at best, humanly prefabricated.

Chittister (2000: p.154)

In the beginning was the creative energy:
And the creative energy was with God
And the creative energy was God...
And it was with God in the beginning....

Fox (1983: p.40)

[God] is the fellow great sufferer who understands.

Whitehead (1929: p.496)

...the word or symbol "God" has generally referred to one, supreme, or holy being, the unity of ultimate reality and ultimate goodness. So conceived, God is believed to have created the entire universe, to rule over it, and to intend to bring it to its fulfillment or realization, to "save" it.

Gilkey (1985: pp.89–90)

I have come to believe that, whether we acknowledge it or not, we all function with one of two images of God: the God of life who accompanies us or an omnipotent God who determines everything.

Soelle (2001: p.11)

God is nothing other than the eternally creative source of relational power, our common strength, a God whose movement is to empower, bringing us into our own together, a God whose name in history is love....

Heyward (1984: p.124)

(quotes continued on next page)

Quotes *(continued)*

The reality of God is like a sea. Isolated from reality, we are like people standing on the shore.

Main (2002: p.131)

While any God worthy of the name is by definition far beyond reason's total grasp, nevertheless a faith that will not stand rational scrutiny, that contradicts reason in any fundamental way, is not a faith for human beings. True spiritual belief is never "blind."

Harpur (1996: pp.18–19)

My Notes

Suggested Reading for Further Exploration

Armstrong, Karen, *The Battle for God: Fundamentalism in Judaism, Christianity and Islam* (Toronto: HarperCollins Publishers Canada Ltd., 2001).

Borg, Marcus J., and Ross Mackenzie, eds., *God at 2000* (Harrisburg, PA: Morehouse Publishing, 2000).

Fox, Matthew, *Original Blessing: A Primer in Creation Spirituality* (Putnam Publishing Group, 2000).

Harpur, Tom, *Would You Believe?: Finding God Without Losing Your Mind* (Toronto: McClelland & Stewart, 1996).

O'Donohue, John, *Anam Cara: A Book of Celtic Wisdom* (New York: HarperCollins, 1998).

O'Murchu, Diarmuid, *Reclaiming Spirituality: A New Spiritual Framework for Today's World* (New York: Crossroad Publishing Company, 1998).

O'Murchu, Diarmuid, *Evolutionary Faith: Rediscovering God in Our Great Story* (Maryknoll, NY: Orbis Books, 2002).

Rupp, Joyce, *The Cosmic Dance: An Invitation to Experience Our Oneness* (Maryknoll, NY: Orbis Books, 2002).

Soelle, Dorothee, Rumscheidt, Barbara and Martin Rumscheidt, trans., *Against the Wind: Memoirs of a Radical Christian* (Minneapolis: Augsburg Fortress, 1999).

Question 3

Who is Jesus for you?

Meeting Format

Meal

Gathering Time

Opening

Check-in

Spiritual Practices/Prayer:
Praying with Scripture: Matthew 15:21-28

Theme Exploration:
Jesus

Checkout

Closing

Suggested Praying with Scripture passage: Matthew 15:21-28

Jesus left that place and went away to the district of Tyre and Sidon. Just then a Canaanite woman from that region came out and started shouting, "Have mercy on me, Lord, Son of David; my daughter is tormented by a demon." But he did not answer her at all. And his disciples came and urged him, saying, "Send her away, for she keeps shouting after us." He answered, "I was sent only to the lost sheep of the house of Israel." But she came and knelt before him, saying, "Lord, help me." He answered, "It is not fair to take the children's food and throw it to the dogs." She said, "Yes, Lord, yet even the dogs eat the crumbs that fall from their masters' table." Then Jesus answered her, "Woman, great is your faith! Let it be done for you as you wish." And her daughter was healed instantly.

See page 155 for information on Praying with Scripture.

Personal Exploration

What words or images, whether positive or challenging, do you associate with the word below? Explore the feelings that they evoke and some of the experiences attached to them.

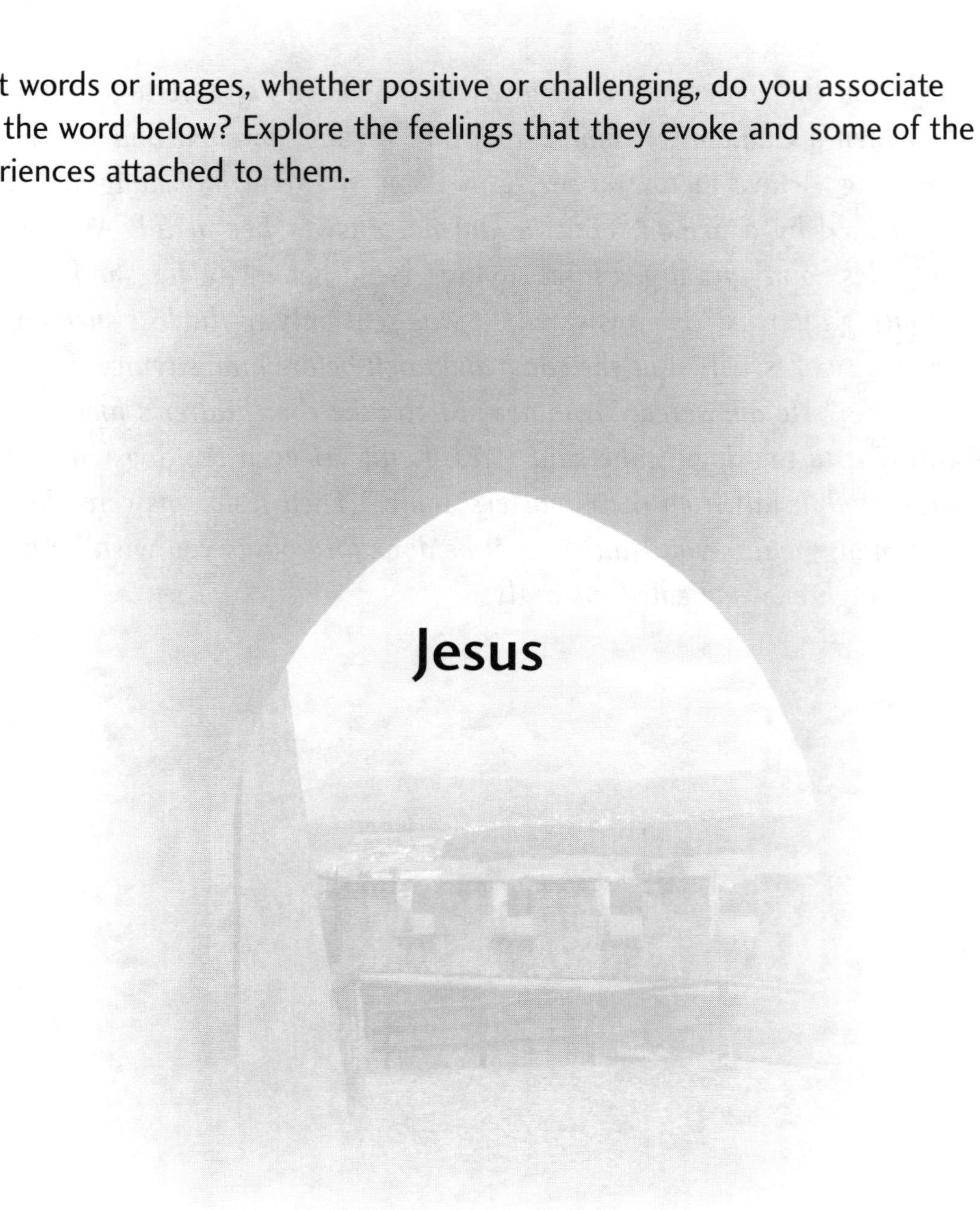

Jesus

How has your understanding or experience of Jesus changed over the years?

How have these changes affected the way you live in the world and how you engage in holistic stewardship*?

*See definition on page 10.

Who is Jesus for you?

He said to them, "But who do you say that I am?"

Matthew 16:15

But when the disciples saw him walking on the sea, they were terrified, saying,
"It is a ghost!" And they cried out in fear.
But immediately Jesus spoke to them and said,
"Take heart, it is I; do not be afraid."

Matthew 14:26–27

Suggested Group Questions:

Who is Jesus for you?
How does your understanding of Jesus relate to your personal faith journey?
How does your understanding of Jesus affect the way you live?

Group Exploration

Turn to the quotes on the following pages. Read each one slowly. Members of your group may wish to take turns reading them out loud. Pause after reading each one to note any thoughts or emotions. Here are some questions to think about:

Does the quote inspire, surprise, anger, confuse, console, amuse, or leave you cold?
What issues, questions, or concerns does the quote raise?
How does the quote relate to your own personal experiences?

Quotes

Jesus embodies as much of the nature of God as you can embody in a human being. I see Jesus as coming from God, revealing part of the nature of God. But he did not reveal all of God. The God of the Bible is never completely known or understood yet is as intimate and compassionate as the most loving parent. If anyone says Jesus represents all of God, I think that's heretical.

Phipps (1997: p.29)

When an abused woman was asked why she did not apply for help she replied: "I did. Early in our marriage I went to a clergyman who, after a few visits, told me that my husband meant no harm, that he was confused, and felt insecure. I was encouraged to be more tolerant and understanding. More important, I was told to forgive the beating just as Christ has forgiven me with the Cross. I did that too."

Martin (1970: p.2)

If the central symbol of Christianity contains with it a message that keeps women impaled on the cross, with societal approval, what message of resurrected hope and redemption can it bring?

Grey (1990: pp.16–17)

In the Christian tradition we are led to the source of our being by a guide, and our guide is Jesus, the fully realized [person], the [person] wholly open to God.

Main (2002: p.79)

But who is Christ for us? How would we tell the Christ story if Jesus had been a reality of this contemporary period of human history?

Spong (1992: p.233)

(quotes continued on next page)

Quotes *(continued)*

The experience of Jesus was an experience of love. This love was a powerful life-affirming reality. It was the love that broke every human barrier and that swept over every human prejudice. It was the love that could not be confined by the Jewish limits in which it was born. It embraced the Syro-Phoenician woman and the Samaritan. It was love that put human life before religious rules (The Sabbath was made for man, not man for the Sabbath). It was love that transcended the religious definitions of what was thought to be clean and unclean. Not only gentiles but lepers, prostitutes, tax collectors, and thieves were transformed with the power of that love.

Spong (1992: pp.237–8)

We ought not participate in a social or religious order constructed on the blood sacrifice of anyone for the common good. Nor should we worship a God who legitimates it. We should rather be struggling to expunge from our spirituality and politics the patriarchal logic that such sacrifice is good for us or others. We must do this if we hope to be non-violent people. None of us, including Jesus, needs to be destroyed so that the rest of us can live holy lives.

Heyward (1999: p.178)

The truth, I have discovered, is that [the] inner experience of the power and presence of God as the Christ within our own consciousness is the best proof of the authenticity of true Christianity. As a scholar friend of mine puts it, "I don't need an external allegedly historical figure to experience God. But I do need the story of Jesus, the mythos, to bring home to me in power the meaning and struggle of my own soul."

Harpur (2004: p.176)

My Notes

Suggested Reading for Further Exploration

Borg, Marcus J., and N.T. Wright, *The Meaning of Jesus: Two Visions* (Toronto: HarperCollins Publishers, 1999).

Gateley, Edwina, and Robert Lentz, *Christ in the Margins* (Maryknoll, NY: Orbis Books, 2003).

Haight, Roger, *Jesus, Symbol of God* (Maryknoll, NY: Orbis, 2000).

Harpur, Tom, *The Pagan Christ: Rediscovering the Lost Light* (Toronto: Thomas Allen Publishers, 2004).

Kuster, Volker, *The Many Faces of Jesus Christ: Intercultural Christology* (Maryknoll, NY: Orbis, 2000).

Nolan, Albert, *Jesus Before Christianity: 25th Anniversary Edition* (Maryknoll, NY: Orbis Books, 2001).

Nouwen, Henri, *Jesus: A Gospel* (Maryknoll, NY: Orbis Books, 2001).

Taussig, Hal, *Jesus Before God: The Prayer Life of the Historical Jesus* (Santa Rosa, CA: Polebridge Press, 1999).

Wessels, Cletus, *Jesus in the New Universe Story* (Maryknoll, NY: Orbis, 2003).

Question 4

The Bible: What does it mean to you?

Meeting Format

Meal

Gathering Time

Opening

Check-in

Spiritual Practices/Prayer:
Praying with Scripture: Matthew 12:1-8

Theme Exploration:
The Bible

Checkout

Closing

Suggested Praying with Scripture passage: Matthew 12:1-8

At that time Jesus went through the grainfields on the sabbath; his disciples were hungry, and they began to pluck heads of grain and to eat. When the Pharisees saw it, they said to him, "Look, your disciples are doing what is not lawful to do on the sabbath." He said to them, "Have you not read what David did when he and his companions were hungry? He entered the house of God and ate the bread of the Presence, which it was not lawful for him or his companions to eat, but only for the priests. Or have you not read in the law that on the sabbath the priests in the temple break the sabbath and yet are guiltless? I tell you, something greater than the temple is here. But if you had known what this means, 'I desire mercy and not sacrifice,' you would not have condemned the guiltless. For the Son of Man is lord of the sabbath."

See page 155 for information on Praying with Scripture.

Personal Exploration

What words or images, whether positive or challenging, do you associate with the phrase below? Explore the feelings that they evoke and some of the experiences attached to them.

The Bible

How has your understanding of the Bible changed over the years?

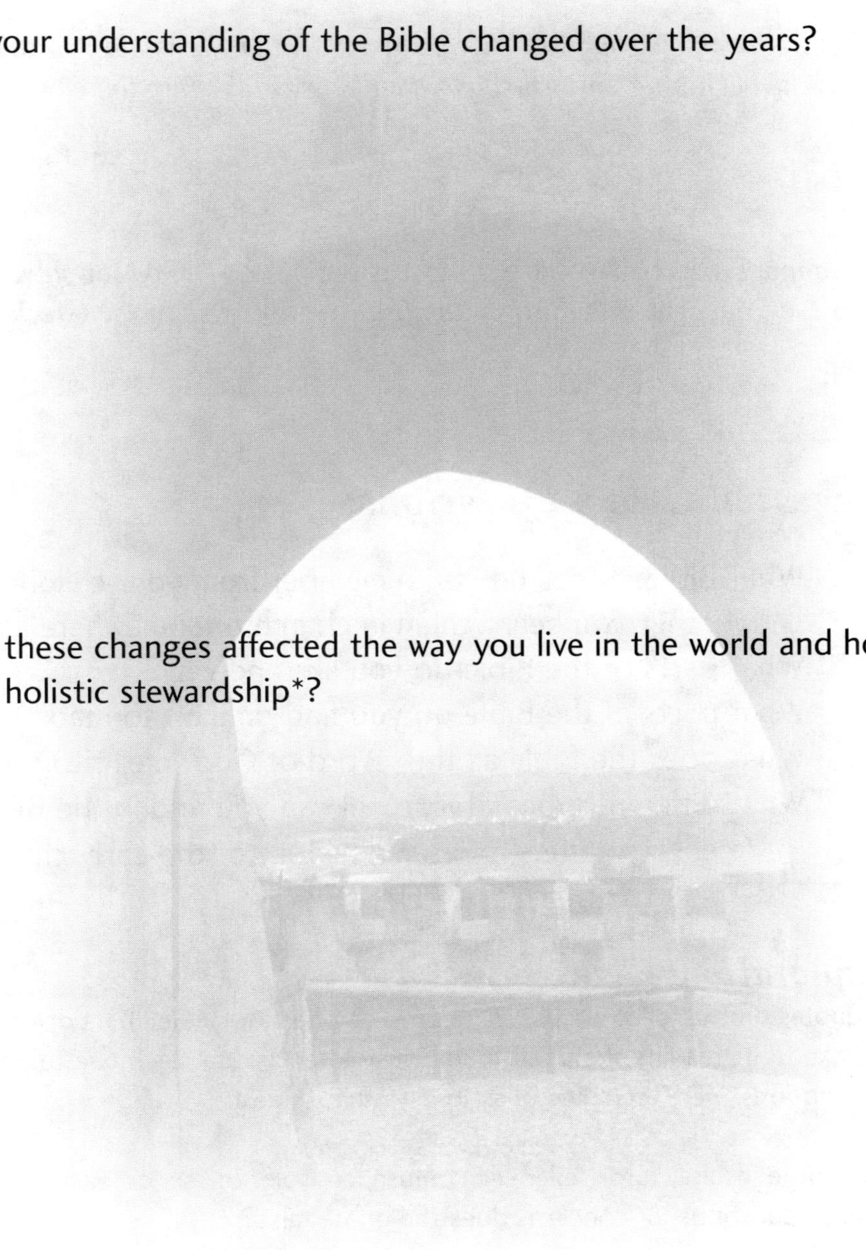

How have these changes affected the way you live in the world and how you engage in holistic stewardship*?

*See definition on page 10.

The Bible: What does it mean to you?

In the first book, Theophilus, I wrote about all that Jesus did and taught from the beginning until the day when he was taken up to heaven…

Acts 1:1–2

For I am not ashamed of the gospel; it is the power of God for salvation to everyone who has faith, to the Jew first and also to the Greek.

Romans 1:16

Suggested Group Questions:

What Bible stories do you remember from your childhood, whether you heard them in church or somewhere else?
What parts of the Bible do you like and why?
What parts of the Bible do you find difficult to read?
What does the Bible as the "Word of God" mean to you?
What different types of material can you find in the Bible (e.g. laws, letters, poetry, a history of the early church, etc.)?

Group Exploration

Turn to the quotes on the following pages. Read each one slowly. Members of your group may wish to take turns reading them out loud. Pause after reading each one to note any thoughts or emotions. Here are some questions to think about:

Does the quote inspire, surprise, anger, confuse, console, amuse, or leave you cold?
What issues, questions, or concerns does the quote raise?
How does the quote relate to your own personal experiences?

Quotes

The biography of a spiritual teacher is not an account of historical facts.... It is a symbol of the spiritual biography of that [person], and all elements of the biography are symbolic. Just through reading them properly you learn the message.

Campbell (1989: p.39)

Conflict about the Bible is the single most divisive issue among Christians in North America today.

Borg (2002: p. ix)

As we enter into the twenty-first century, we need a new set of lenses through which to read the Bible. The older set, ground and polished by modernity, no longer works for millions of people. These lenses need to be replaced. The older way of seeing and reading the Bible...has made the Bible incredible and irrelevant for vast numbers of people. This is so not only for the millions who have left the church in Europe and North America, but also for many Christians who continue to be active in the life of the church.

Borg (2002: pp.3–4)

The Bible relates to us the way our ancient forbears understood and interpreted their world, made sense out of life and thought about God. Our task is the same as theirs. We must interpret our world in light of our knowledge and suppositions.

Spong (1992: p.33)

It might be interesting to speculate upon the probable length of a "depatriarchalized Bible." Perhaps there would be enough salvageable material to comprise an interesting pamphlet.

Daly (1973: p.206)

The Spirit speaks to our conscience through scripture and through the events of daily life.

Keating (1997: p.17)

(quotes continued on next page)

Quotes *(continued)*

When people live under oppressive structures, they turn to the Bible for the strength to survive another day not to figure out how long a day lasted in Genesis 1.

de la Torre (2002: p.40)

My Notes

Suggested Reading for Further Exploration

Borg, Marcus J., *Reading the Bible Again for the First Time: Taking the Bible Seriously but Not Literally* (New York: HarperCollins Publishers, 2001).

de la Torre, Miguel, A., *Reading the Bible from the Margins* (Maryknoll, NY: Orbis Books, 2002).

Harpur, Tom, *The Pagan Christ: Rediscovering the Lost Light* (Toronto: Thomas Allen Publishers, 2004).

Howard-Brook, Wes, and Sharon H. Ringe, eds., *The New Testament: Introducing the Way of Discipleship* (Maryknoll, NY: Orbis Books, 2002).

McAfee Brown, Robert, *Unexpected News: Reading the Bible with Third World Eyes* (Louisville, KY: Westminster John Knox Press, 1984).

Schussler Fiorenza, Elisabeth, *Wisdom Ways: Introducing Feminist Biblical Interpretation* (Maryknoll, NY: Orbis Books, 2001).

Shelby Spong, John, *Rescuing the Bible from Fundamentalism: A Bishop Rethinks the Meaning of Scripture* (Toronto: HarperCollins Publishers Canada, 1992).

Question 5

Prayer: What does it mean to you?

Meeting Format

Meal

Gathering Time

Opening

Check-in

Spiritual Practices/Prayer:
Praying with Scripture: Luke 11:9-13

Theme Exploration:
Prayer

Checkout

Closing

Suggested Praying with Scripture passage: Luke 11:9-13

"So I say to you, Ask, and it will be given you; search, and you will find; knock, and the door will be opened for you. For everyone who asks receives, and everyone who searches finds, and for everyone who knocks, the door will be opened. Is there anyone among you who, if your child asks for a fish, will give a snake instead of a fish? Or if the child asks for an egg, will give a scorpion?

If you then, who are evil, know how to give good gifts to your children, how much more will [God] give the Holy Spirit to those who ask…!"

See page 155 for information on Praying with Scripture.

Personal Exploration

What words or images, whether positive or challenging, do you associate with the word below? Explore the feelings that they evoke and some of the experiences attached to them.

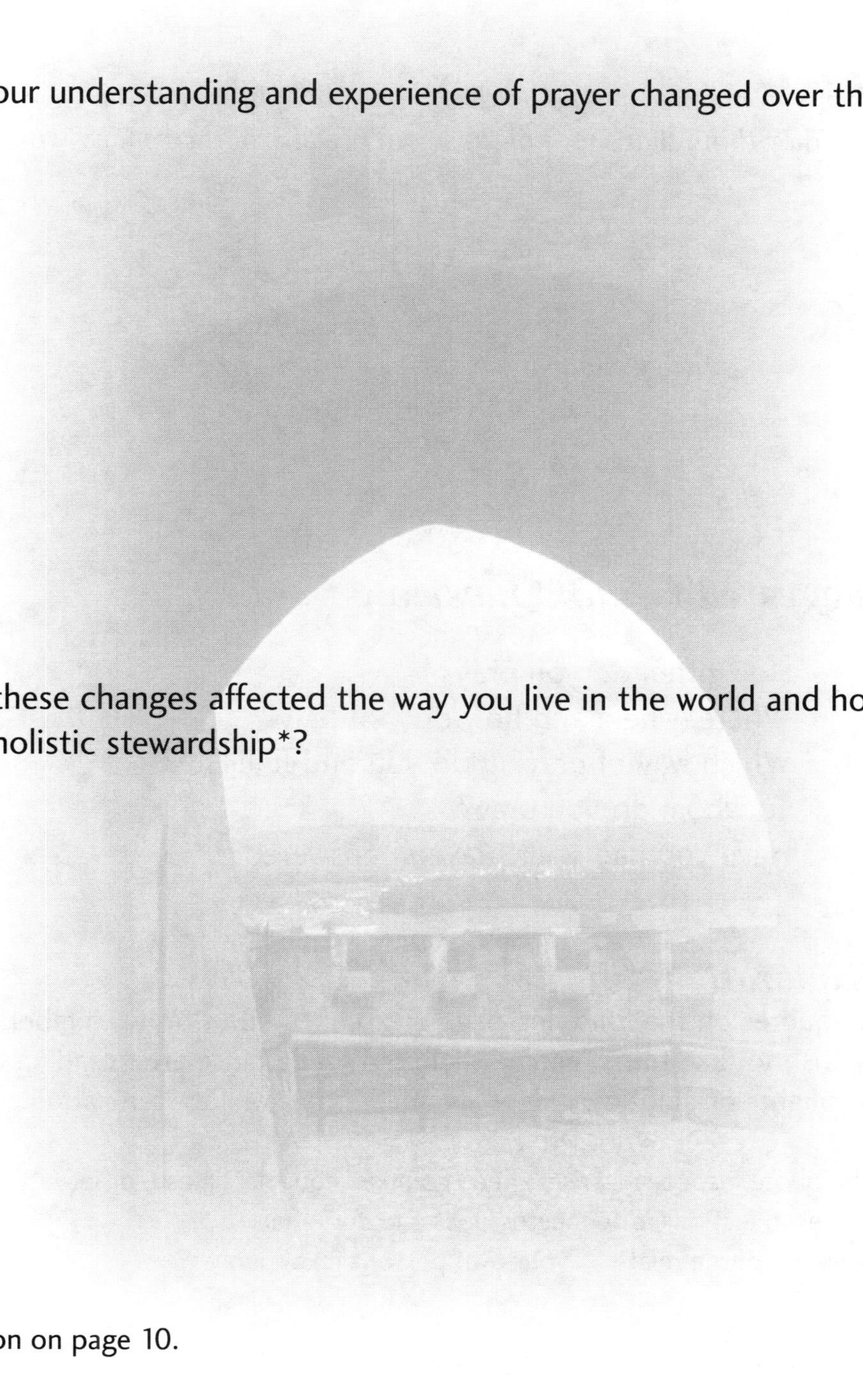

How has your understanding and experience of prayer changed over the years?

How have these changes affected the way you live in the world and how you engage in holistic stewardship*?

*See definition on page 10.

Prayer: What does it mean to you?

"When you are praying, do not heap up empty phrases as the Gentiles do; for they think that they will be heard because of their many words."

Matthew 6:7

In the morning, while it was still very dark,
he got up and went out to a deserted place,
and there he prayed.

Mark 1:35

Suggested Group Questions:

How often do you pray?
Where, when, and how do you pray?
Which way of praying do you find fulfilling?
To whom do you pray?
Have you had your prayers "answered"?

Group Exploration

Turn to the quotes on the following page. Read each one slowly. Members of your group may wish to take turns reading them out loud. Pause after reading each one to note any thoughts or emotions. Here are some questions to think about:

Does the quote inspire, surprise, anger, confuse, console, amuse, or leave you cold?
What issues, questions, or concerns does the quote raise?
How does the quote relate to your own personal experiences?

Quotes

Prayer is not primarily saying or thinking thoughts. It is, rather, a stance. It's a way of living in the Presence. It is further a way of living in the awareness of the Presence, even enjoying the Presence. The full contemplative is not just aware of the Presence, but trusts, allows, and delights in it.

Rohr (1999: p.29)

I am now persuaded that speaking to God from your heart is the only real religious issue there is. Learn to pray, and all else follows. It is not the content of the heart that matters, only the ability to speak from it. We sometimes think that a heart full of hatred, or envy, or a heart drained of passion, disqualifies itself for authentic prayer. The task, however, is not preparing your heart for prayer, but speaking from your heart as it is.

Carse (1995: p.2)

If we knew how to listen to God, if we knew how to look around us, our whole life would become prayer.

Quoist (1963: p.30)

An inner journey is altogether healthy and necessary—we take inner journeys into ourselves, into our loved ones, into trees, into Mozart's music, into death, into pain and suffering and injustice, ideally all the time. To pray is to enter in, thus to make an inner journey. But a person who takes an inward journey looks only into himself or herself for God or for spiritual refreshment. It is introspection. There lies the death of cosmic spirituality, the death of cosmos, and the excessive quest for personal salvation. The world does not need more inward journeys; but there are no limits to the inner journeys we can make.

Fox (1983: p.77)

Contemplative prayer is a process of interior transformation, a conversation initiated by God and leading, if we consent, to divine union.

Keating (1997: p.4)

My Notes

Suggested Reading for Further Exploration

Carse, James P., *The Silence of God: Meditations on Prayer* (Toronto: HarperCollins Publishers Canada, 1995).

Collins, Pat, *Prayer in Practice* (Maryknoll, NY: Orbis Books, 2001).

Keating, Thomas, *Open Mind, Open Heart: The Contemplative Dimension of the Gospel* (New York: Continuum, 2002).

Keating, Thomas, *Invitation to Love: The Way of Christian Contemplation* (New York: Continuum International Publishing Group, 1994).

Mathis, Rick, *Prayer-Centered Healing: Finding the God Who Heals* (Liguori, Missouri: Liguori Publications, 2000).

Reininger, Gustave, ed., *Centering Prayer in Daily Life and Ministry* (New York: Continuum International Publishing Group, 1997).

Skinner Sawyers, June, *Praying with Celtic Saints, Prophets, Martyrs and Poets* (Chicago, IL: Sheed & Ward, 2004).

Question 6

How can we talk about God and suffering?

Meeting Format

Meal

Gathering Time

Opening

Check-in

Spiritual Practices/Prayer:
Praying with Scripture: Luke 13:10-17

Theme Exploration:
God and Suffering

Checkout

Closing

Suggested Praying with Scripture passage: Luke 13:10-17

Now he was teaching in one of the synagogues on the sabbath. And just then there appeared a woman with a spirit that had crippled her for eighteen years. She was bent over and was quite unable to stand up straight. When Jesus saw her, he called her over and said, "Woman, you are set free from your ailment." When he laid his hands on her, immediately she stood up straight and began praising God. But the leader of the synagogue, indignant because Jesus had cured on the sabbath, kept saying to the crowd, "There are six days on which work ought to be done; come on those days and be cured, and not on the sabbath day." But the Lord answered him and said, "You hypocrites! Does not each of you on the sabbath untie his ox or his donkey from the manger, and lead it away to give it water? And ought not this woman, a daughter of Abraham whom Satan bound for eighteen long years, be set free from this bondage on the sabbath day?" When he said this, all his opponents were put to shame; and the entire crowd was rejoicing at all the wonderful things that he was doing.

See page 155 for information on Praying with Scripture.

Personal Exploration

What words or images, whether positive or challenging, do you associate with the phrase below? Explore the feelings that they evoke and some of the experiences attached to them.

God and Suffering

How has your understanding of God and suffering changed over the years?

How have these changes affected the way you live in the world and how you engage in holistic stewardship*?

*See definition on page 10.

How can we talk about God and suffering?

I am weary with my moaning; every night I flood my bed with tears;
I drench my couch with my weeping. My eyes waste away because of grief;
they grow weak because of all my foes.

Psalm 6:6–7

When it was noon, darkness came over the whole land, until three in the afternoon. At three o'clock, Jesus cried with a loud voice, "Eloi, Eloi, lama sabachthani?" which means, "My God, my God, why have you forsaken me?" …Then Jesus gave a loud cry and breathed his last. And the curtain of the temple was torn in two, from top to bottom.

Mark 15:33–34, 37–38

Suggested Group Questions:

How do you reconcile the following statements? God is good. Whether we like it or not, suffering is part of life.

How has your personal suffering or that of others changed the way you understand God?

Is suffering necessary?

How does your understanding of God and suffering affect how you act in the world?

Group Exploration

Turn to the quotes on the following pages. Read each one slowly. Members of your group may wish to take turns reading them out loud. Pause after reading each one to note any thoughts or emotions. Here are some questions to think about:

Does the quote inspire, surprise, anger, confuse, console, amuse, or leave you cold?
What issues, questions, or concerns does the quote raise?
How does the quote relate to your own personal experiences?

Quotes

When I can no longer bear my loneliness I take it to my friends. For I must share it with all friends of God. "Do you suffer?" "So do I."

Mechtild of Magdeburg, quoted in Fox (1983: p.145)

There can be no human beings who are completely alone in their sufferings since God, in and through Jesus, has become Emmanuel, God with us. It belongs to the centre of our faith that God is a faithful God, a God who did not want us ever to be alone but who wanted to understand—to stand under—all that is human. The Good News of the Gospel, therefore is not that God came to take our suffering away, but that God wanted to become part of it.

Nouwen (1998: p.111)

The great secret of life is how to survive struggle without succumbing to it, how to bear struggle without being defeated by it, how to come out of great struggle better than when we found ourselves in the midst of it.

Chittister (2003: p.13)

...the evidence of evolution seems to suggest that God does not have a problem with the suffering and destruction that are innate to the unfolding process. We humans have a problem with it, but God does not. This is not to say that all suffering is meaningful at one level or another. Hidden, mysterious meaning covers a good deal of it; more of it is obviously horrendous and in no way could be willed by God—for example, the slaughter of almost one million people in Rwanda in 1994. In this latter case, the meaningless face of suffering, there is overwhelming evidence to suggest that it is caused by human beings, and not by the capricious nature of life, whether understood in secular or religious terms.

O'Murchu (2002: pp.105–6)

(quotes continued on next page)

Quotes *(continued)*

The poet Rainer Maria Rilke, who himself underwent a profoundly painful childhood, having been locked in the attic by his mother for long periods of time, and having been sent to a military school even though he was a sensitive child, learned something of praise and pleasure from his journeys into pain. He writes:

> Oh, tell us, poet, what do you do? I praise.
> But the deadly and the violent days,
> How do you undergo them, take them in? I praise.
> But the namelessness—how do you raise
> That, invoke the unnameable? I praise.
> What right have you, through every phrase,
> In every mask, to remain true? I praise.
> —and that both stillness and the wild affray
> know you, like star and storm? Because I praise.

Fox (1983: p.144)

My Notes

Suggested Reading for Further Exploration

Cejka, Mary Ann, and Thomas Bamat, eds., *Artisans of Peace: Grassroots Peacemaking among Christian Communities* (Maryknoll, NY: Orbis Books, 2003).

Chittister, Joan, *Scarred by Struggle, Transformed by Hope* (Grand Rapids, MI.: William B. Eerdmans, 2003).

Ellis, Marc H., *Unholy Alliance: Religion and Atrocity in Our Time* (Minneapolis: Fortress Press, 1997).

Ortiz, Dianna, and Patricia Davis, *The Blindfold's Eyes: My Journey from Torture to Truth* (Maryknoll, NY: Orbis Books, 2002).

Smith-Christopher, Daniel L., ed., *Subverting Hatred: The Challenge of Nonviolence in Religious Traditions* (Maryknoll, NY: Orbis Books, 2002).

Soelle, Dorothee, *Suffering* (Minneapolis: Augsburg Fortress Publishers, 1975).

Tamez, Elsa et al., eds. *Women Resisting Violence: Spirituality for Life* (Maryknoll, NY: Orbis Books, 1996).

Vanier, Jean, *The Broken Body: Journey to Wholeness* (Toronto: Anglican Book Centre, 1988).

Walters, Kerry, *Jacob's Hip: Finding God in an Anxious Age* (Maryknoll, NY: Orbis Books, 2003).

Question 7

Who me, a sinner?

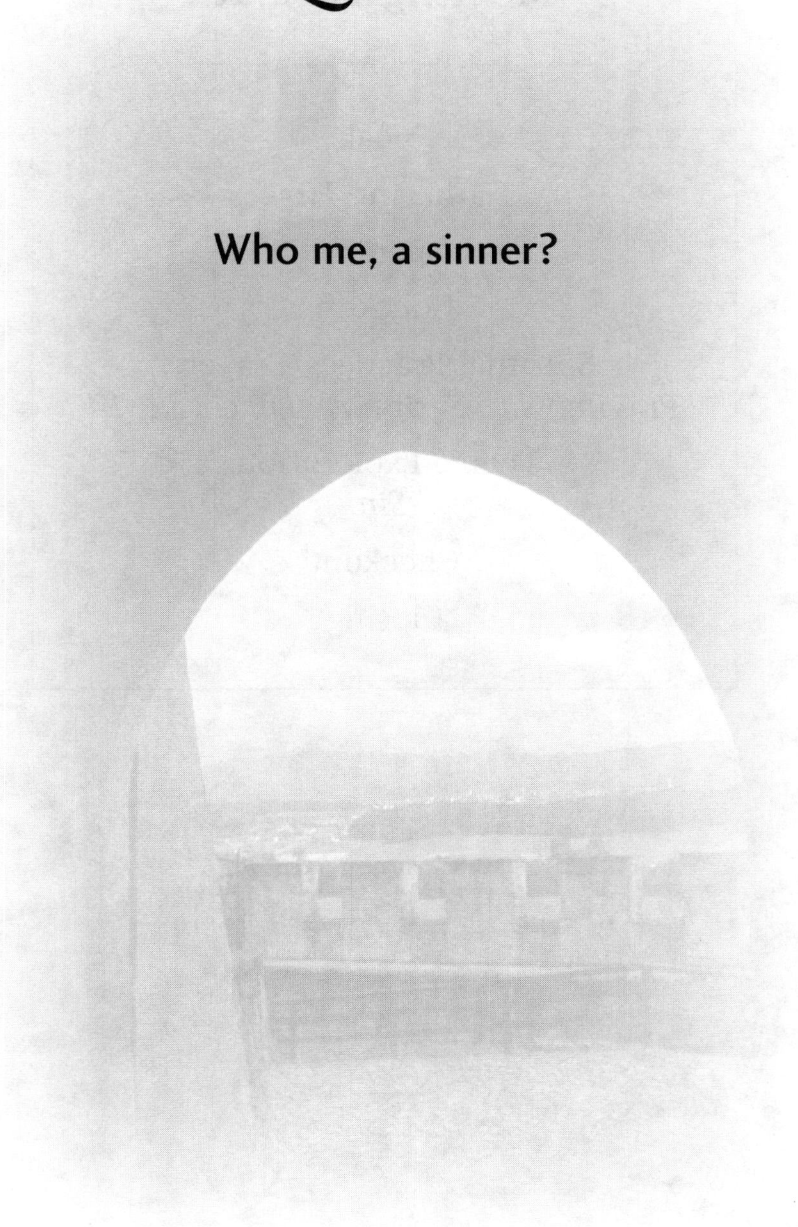

Meeting Format

Meal

Gathering Time

Opening

Check-in

Spiritual Practices/Prayer:
Praying with Scripture: Luke 18:9-14

Theme Exploration:
Sin

Checkout

Closing

Suggested Praying with Scripture passage: Luke 18:9-14

He also told this parable to some who trusted in themselves that they were righteous and regarded others with contempt: "Two men went up to the temple to pray, one a Pharisee and the other a tax collector. The Pharisee, standing by himself, was praying thus, 'God, I thank you that I am not like other people: thieves, rogues, adulterers, or even like this tax collector. I fast twice a week; I give a tenth of all my income.' But the tax collector, standing far off, would not even look up to heaven, but was beating his breast and saying, 'God, be merciful to me, a sinner!' I tell you, this man went down to his home justified rather than the other; for all who exalt themselves will be humbled, but all who humble themselves will be exalted."

See page 155 for information on Praying with Scripture.

Personal Exploration

What words or images, whether positive or challenging, do you associate with the word below? Explore the feelings that they evoke and some of the experiences attached to them.

Sin

How has your understanding of sin changed over the years?

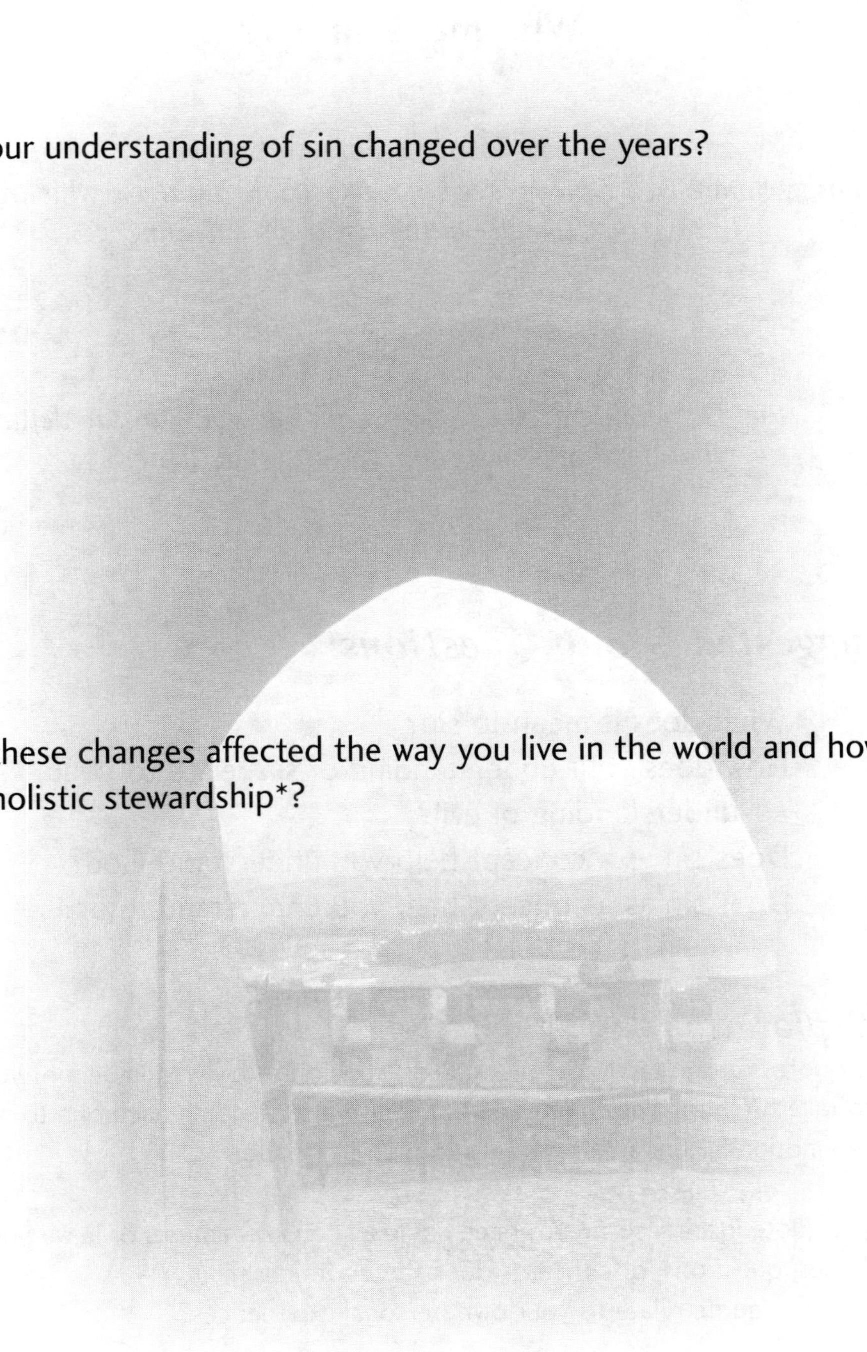

How have these changes affected the way you live in the world and how you engage in holistic stewardship*?

*See definition on page 10.

Who me, a sinner?

When Jesus heard this he said to them,
"Those who are well have no need of a physician, but those who are sick;
I have come to call not the righteous but sinners."

Mark 2:17

"...there is nothing outside a person that by going in can defile,
but the things that come out are what defile."

Mark 7:15

Suggested Group Questions:

What does it mean to sin?
How does your understanding of sin relate to your understanding of evil?
Does sin as a concept help you understand God?
Does sin as a concept help you understand Jesus?

Group Exploration

Turn to the quotes on the following pages. Read each one slowly. Members of your group may wish to take turns reading them out loud. Pause after reading each one to note any thoughts or emotions. Here are some questions to think about:

Does the quote inspire, surprise, anger, confuse, console, amuse, or leave you cold?
What issues, questions, or concerns does the quote raise?
How does the quote relate to your own personal experiences?

Quotes

A helpful definition of sin defines sin as the failure to love as we were created to love.

Noe (2001: p.16)

[Our] capacity for evil, then, is less a positive capacity, for all its horrendous activity, than a failure to develop [our] most human function, the imagination, to its fullness, and consequently a failure to develop compassion.

Levertov (1973: p.53)

The sin against the Holy Spirit is the sin against new life, against self-emergence, against the Holy fecund innerness of each person. It can be committed quite as easily against oneself as against another.

Richards (1964: p.59)

Where art has no role to play in education, religion, science, the media, and where it has been replaced by entertainment, sin abounds. Sins of unemployment, boredom, and the violence that accompanies boredom. Loss of art is a social sin. With that deprivation our work life becomes distorted and violent, and so does our leisure time.

Fox (1983: p.234)

Sin changes with age. In youth it is born out of impulse; in later years it is based in calculation. The first stage requires the ability to discriminate and the development of control. It's a period of experimentation that can end in wisdom. But at a later stage, when we have really come to "know good from evil," sin requires that we review the entire value system that drives us. Something has gone seriously awry. And in the end it is not just what our sin does to other people that counts; it is what sin does to us that matters deeply as well.

Chittister (2000: p.141)

(quotes continued on next page)

Quotes *(continued)*

Social sin is the systemic embodiment of distorted relationality that issues from personal sin. Because it is built into social structures and institutions, it takes on a life of its own, aside from individual egoism, passivity and self-centeredness.

Snyder (1988: pp.109–110)

Good can always come out of evil. But evil is no way to achieve good. Stooping to the level of the inhuman to do good does nothing to humanize the world.

Chittister (2000: p.140)

Annie Dillard tells a story about a tribesman who said to the missionary, "If I did not know about God and sin, would I go to hell?" And the priest said to the tribesman, "Oh no, if you didn't know about God and sin, God would not send you to hell." "Then, why," the tribesman said, "did you tell me?"

Chittister (2000: p.143)

My Notes

Suggested Reading for Further Exploration

Argueta, Manlio, *One Day of Life* (New York:Vintage Books, 1991).

Mosionier, Beatrice, and Cheryl Suzack, ed., *In Search of April Raintree: Critical Edition* (Winnipeg: Portage and Main Press, 1999).

Nelson, Susan L., *Healing the Broken Heart: Sin, Alienation, and the Gift of Grace* (St. Louis, MO: Chalice Press, 1997).

Spong, John Shelby, *Living in Sin: A Bishop Rethinks Sexuality* (Scarborough: HarperCollins, 1990).

Suchocki, Marjorie H., *The Fall to Violence: Original Sin in Relational Theology* (New York: Continuum International Publishing Group, 1995).

Taylor, James, *Sin: A New Understanding of Virtue and Vice* (Kelowna, BC: Northstone Publishing, 1997).

Question 8

Forgiveness: What are the challenges and the blessings?

Meeting Format

Meal

Gathering Time

Opening

Check-in

Spiritual Practices/Prayer:
Praying with Scripture: Luke 5:27-32

Theme Exploration:
Forgiveness

Checkout

Closing

Suggested Praying with Scripture passage: Luke 5:27-32

After this he went out and saw a tax collector named Levi, sitting at the tax booth; and he said to him, "Follow me." And he got up, left everything, and followed him. Then Levi gave a great banquet for him in his house; and there was a large crowd of tax collectors and others sitting at the table with them. The Pharisees and their scribes were complaining to his disciples, saying, "Why do you eat and drink with tax collectors and sinners?" Jesus answered, "Those who are well have no need of a physician, but those who are sick; I have come to call not the righteous but sinners to repentance."

See page 155 for information on Praying with Scripture.

Personal Exploration

What words or images, whether positive or challenging, do you associate with the word below? Explore the feelings that they evoke and some of the experiences attached to them.

Forgiveness

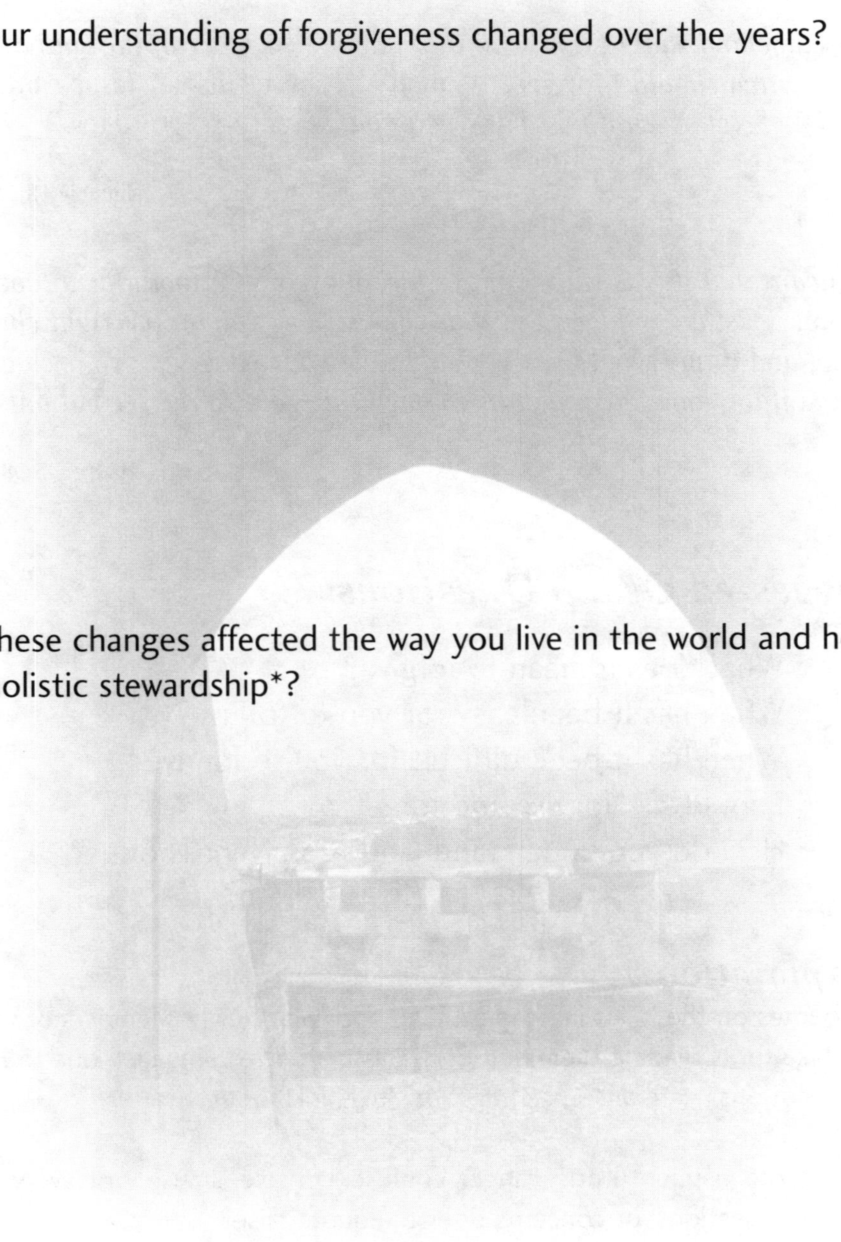

How has your understanding of forgiveness changed over the years?

How have these changes affected the way you live in the world and how you engage in holistic stewardship*?

*See definition on page 10.

Forgiveness: What are the challenges and the blessings?

Then Peter came and said to him, "Lord, if another member of the church sins against me, how often should I forgive? As many as seven times?" Jesus said to him, "Not seven times, but, I tell you, seventy-seven times."

Matthew 18:21–22

"You have heard that it was said, 'An eye for an eye and a tooth for a tooth.' But I say to you, do not resist an evildoer. But if anyone strikes you on the right cheek, turn the other also; and if any would sue you and take your coat, give your cloak as well; and if any one forces you to go one mile, go also the second mile."

Matthew 5:38–41

Suggested Group Questions:

What does it mean to forgive?
When has it been easy for you to forgive?
When has it been difficult for you to forgive?
Should we "forgive and forget"?
How do you understand God's forgiveness of us?

Group Exploration

Turn to the quotes on the following pages. Read each one slowly. Members of your group may wish to take turns reading them out loud. Pause after reading each one to note any thoughts or emotions. Here are some questions to think about:

Does the quote inspire, surprise, anger, confuse, console, amuse, or leave you cold?
What issues, questions, or concerns does the quote raise?
How does the quote relate to your own personal experiences?

Quotes

I don't believe that forgetting is one of the signs of forgiveness. I forgive, but I remember. I do not forget the pain, the loneliness, the ache, the terrible injustice. But I do not remember it to inflict guilt or some future retribution. Having forgiven, I am liberated. I need no longer be determined by the past. I move into the future free to imagine new possibilities.

Jenco (1995: p.135)

Unless we allow ourselves to feel the hurt and to express it, it is unlikely an act of forgiveness will be genuine. If the forgiveness we seek to offer to those who need our forgiveness is to be of use to them, they need to be aware of what they have done and the pain or hurt it has caused.

Jim Forest, as quoted in Jenco (1995: p.135)

While we were there [the Johweto community in South Africa which was formed when white South Africans from Johannesburg and black South Africans from Soweto moved onto a farm to live together in defiance of apartheid and with hopes of bringing healing to their divided nation], Silulama, one of the black members of the Johweto community explained, "I still have a lot of anger toward white South Africans, so much that some days I feel I might explode."

"What keeps you from exploding?" I asked.

"Relationships," he said. "Real relationships are disarming me. I can no longer look at a white person as just the oppressor and not a real person.

Noe (2001: p.40)

Forgiveness means we renounce vengeance and retaliation, but it does not mean passive acquiescence to abuse.

Linn (1997: p.8)

(quotes continued on next page)

Quotes *(continued)*

If you do as the passage [Matthew 5:38–41] says and turn your other cheek (your left cheek) and your master must use his right hand [the left is for unclean tasks], then he can no longer backhand you [a gesture used to humiliate another]. If he hits you again, he will have to use his fist. Hitting another with a fist was a gesture used only between equals. Thus, by turning your other cheek, you have reclaimed your dignity and communicated that you refuse to be humiliated. You have also invited your master to reclaim his true dignity by examining the lie by which he lives, that one human being is better than another. And you have done all this non-violently, without striking back.

Linn (1997: pp.5–6) (See Appendix C for the rest of Linn's commentary on this passage.)

My Notes

Suggested Reading for Further Exploration

Buechner, Frederick, *The Storm* (San Francisco: Harper, 1998).

Cejka, Mary Ann, and Thomas Bamat, eds., *Artisans of Peace: Grassroots Peacemaking among Christian Communities* (Maryknoll, NY: Orbis Books, 2003).

Jenco, Lawrence Martin, *Bound to Forgive: The Pilgrimage to Reconciliation of a Beirut Hostage* (Notre Dame, Indiana: Ave Maria Press, 1995).

Linn, Dennis, Sheila Fabricant Linn, and Matthew Linn, *Don't Forgive Too Soon: Extending the Two Hands That Heal* (New Jersey: Paulist Press, 1997).

Minow, Martha, *Between Vengeance and Forgiveness: Facing History after Genocide and Mass Violence* (Boston: Beacon, 1999).

Shults, F. Le Ron, and Steven J. Sandage, *The Faces of Forgiveness: Searching for Wholeness and Salvation* (Ada, MI: Baker Academic, 2003).

Tutu, Desmond Mpilo, *No Future Without Forgiveness* (New York: Doubleday, 2000).

Wink, Walter, ed., *Peace is the Way: Writings on Nonviolence from the Fellowship of Reconciliation* (Maryknoll, NY: Orbis Books, 2000).

Wink, Walter, *Engaging the Powers: Discernment and Resistance in a World of Domination* (Minneapolis: Fortress Press, 2003).

Question 9

After death: What is next?

Meeting Format

Meal

Gathering Time

Opening

Check-in

Spiritual Practices/Prayer:
Praying with Scripture: 1 Corinthians 13:8-13

Theme Exploration:
Life after Death

Checkout

Closing

Suggested Praying with Scripture passage: 1 Corinthians 13:8-13

Love never ends. But as for prophecies, they will come to an end; as for tongues, they will cease; as for knowledge, it will come to an end. For we know only in part, and we prophesy only in part; but when the complete comes, the partial will come to an end. When I was a child, I spoke like a child, I thought like a child, I reasoned like a child; when I became an adult, I put an end to childish ways.

For now we see in a mirror, dimly, but then we will see face to face. Now I know only in part; then I will know fully, even as I have been fully known. And now faith, hope, and love abide, these three; and the greatest of these is love.

See page 155 for information on Praying with Scripture.

Personal Exploration

What words or images, whether positive or challenging, do you associate with the phrase below? Explore the feelings that they evoke and some of the experiences attached to them.

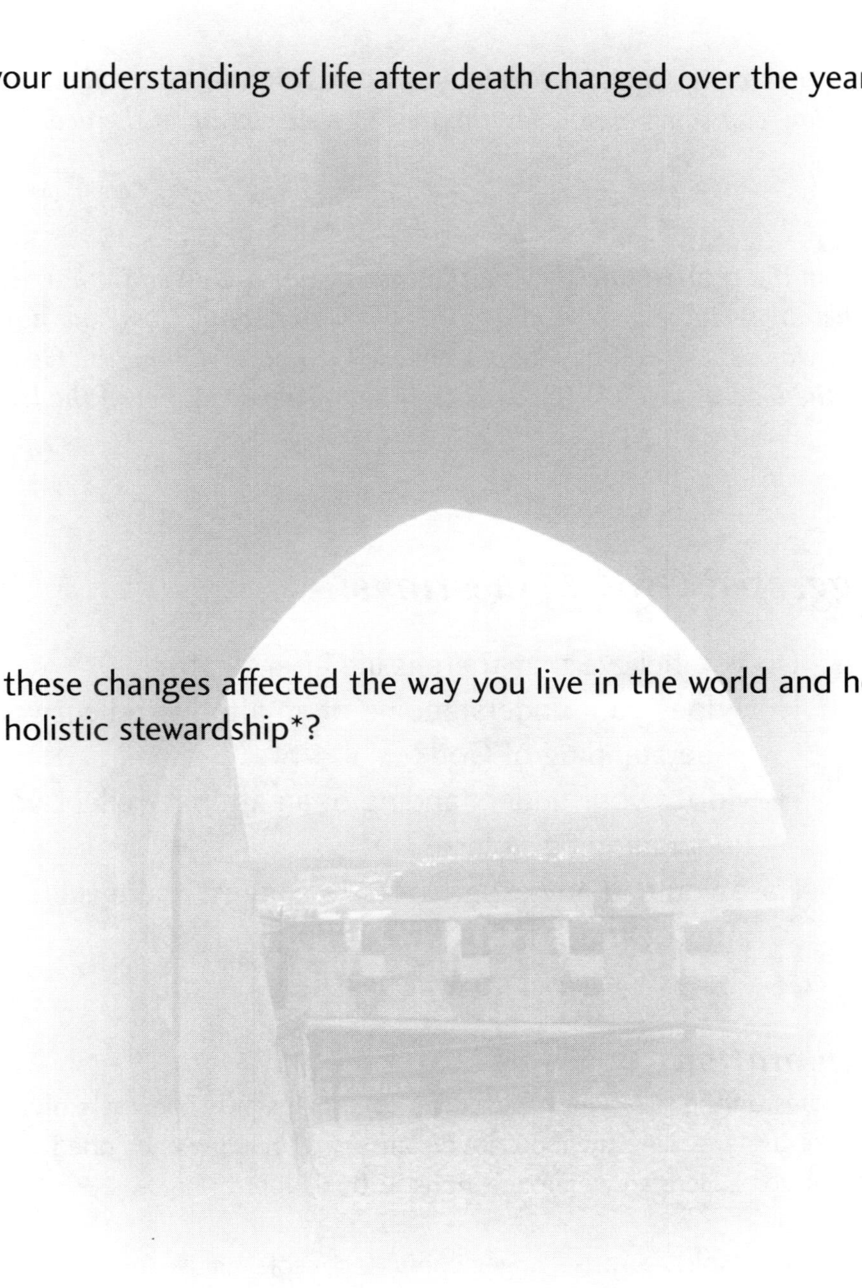

How has your understanding of life after death changed over the years?

How have these changes affected the way you live in the world and how you engage in holistic stewardship*?

*See definition on page 10.

After death: What is next?

Now if Christ is proclaimed as raised from the dead,
how can some of you say there is no resurrection of the dead?

1 Corinthians 15:12

For in the resurrection they neither marry nor are given in marriage,
but are like angels in heaven. And as for the resurrection of the dead, have you not
read what was said to you by God, "I am the God of Abraham, the God of Isaac,
and the God of Jacob"? [God] is God not of the dead, but of the living.

Matthew 22:30–33

Suggested Group Questions:

Do you believe that there is life after death?
How does your understanding of an afterlife reflect your understanding of God?
How does your understanding of an afterlife reflect your understanding of Jesus?
Have you had any experiences to suggest there is life after death?

Group Exploration

Turn to the quotes on the following pages. Read each one slowly. Members of your group may wish to take turns reading them out loud. Pause after reading each one to note any thoughts or emotions. Here are some questions to think about:

Does the quote inspire, surprise, anger, confuse, console, amuse, or leave you cold?
What issues, questions, or concerns does the quote raise?
How does the quote relate to your own personal experiences?

Quotes

Surely the most momentous personal question of our day—or indeed any other—is, having once died, is that the end, or do we somehow live again?

Harpur (1991: p.17)

There is today a major paradox in the fact that, while more people than ever are concerned about dying and what may lie beyond, fewer and fewer turn to traditional religion to find the answers they seek.

Harpur (1991: p.16)

Now I lay me down to sleep.
I pray the Lord my soul to keep.
If I should die before I wake
I pray the Lord my soul to take.

Child's bedtime prayer, 18th century

When the bishop gave me my first parish, out in the "wilds" of Scarborough, Ontario, he sent me a young priest from the Church of South India, who was studying at Wycliffe College to be my Sunday assistant. His name was T.K. George, a small, gentle man of deep faith and intelligence. Just as I was writing this chapter a letter came from a former parishioner of mine saying that she had just heard from T.K.'s wife. She wrote that my former associate had died very peacefully at his home in India after a long illness. What she particularly wanted to share with those who had known him was that, just before the moment of his last breath, he told his wife he could see "my spiritual body coming to meet me."

Harpur (1991: p.45)

The major issue is not immortality per se, but justice, and that the fullness of justice requires a transhistorical dimension through some form of existence beyond death.

Suchocki (1989: p.63)

(quotes continued on next page)

Quotes *(continued)*

The concept of the "immortal self," survivable apart from our particular transient organism must be recognized, not only as untenable, but as the source of much destructive behaviour toward the earth and other humans.

Ruether (1992: p.251)

The eternal world does not seem to be a place but rather a state of being. The soul of the person goes no place because there is no place else to go. This suggests that the dead are here with us, in the air that we are moving through all the time. The only difference between us and the dead is that they are now in an invisible form.... Maybe when a person goes into that world, he or she can look back at what we call past time here. That person may also see all of future time.

O'Donohue (1997: pp.226–227)

My Notes

Suggested Reading for Further Exploration

Harpur, Tom, *Life After Death* (Toronto: McClelland & Stewart, 1992).

Kung, Hans, *Eternal Life* (New York: Herder & Herder, 1991).

Lackey, Douglas P., *God, Immortality, Ethics: A Concise Introduction to Philosophy* (Pacific Grove, CA: Brooks/Cole, 1989).

Sawicki, Marianne, *Seeing the Lord: Resurrection and Early Christian Practices* (Minneapolis: Fortress Press, 2003).

Question 10

Nurturing your faith: Which spiritual practices are best for you?

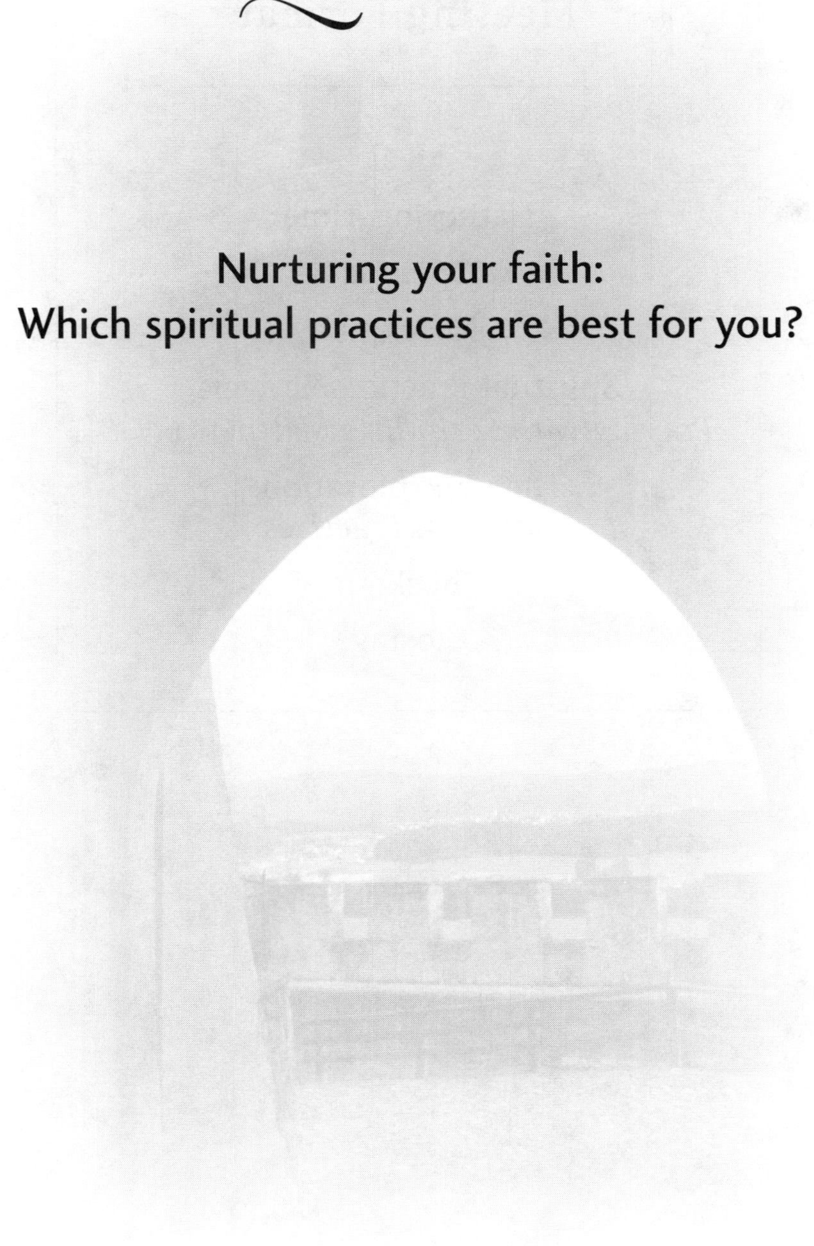

Meeting Format

Meal

Gathering Time

Opening

Check-in

Spiritual Practices/Prayer:
Praying with Scripture: Matthew 6:1-8

Theme Exploration:
Spiritual Practices

Checkout

Closing

Suggested Praying with Scripture passage: Matthew 6:1-8

Beware of practicing your piety before others in order to be seen by them; for then you have no reward from [God] in heaven. So whenever you give alms, do not sound a trumpet before you, as the hypocrites do in the synagogues and in the streets, so that they may be praised by others. Truly I tell you, they have received their reward. But when you give alms, do not let your left hand know what your right hand is doing, so that your alms may be done in secret; and [God] who sees in secret will reward you.

And whenever you pray, do not be like the hypocrites; for they love to stand and pray in the synagogues and at the street corners, so that they may be seen by others. Truly I tell you, they have received their reward. But whenever you pray, go into your room and shut the door and pray to [God] who is in secret; and [God] who sees in secret will reward you.

When you are praying, do not heap up empty phrases as the Gentiles do; for they think that they will be heard because of their many words. Do not be like them, for [God] knows what you need before you ask him.

See page 155 for information on Praying with Scripture.

Personal Exploration

What words or images, whether positive or challenging, do you associate with the phrase below? Explore the feelings that they evoke and some of the experiences attached to them. Spiritual practices are exercises, habits, or disciplines that we carry out on a regular basis to help us develop our spirituality, that is to open ourselves to God. These include, for example, prayer, meditation, walking the labyrinth, and reading scripture.

Spiritual Practices

How has your understanding and experience of spiritual practices changed over the years?

How have these changes affected the way you live in the world and how you engage in holistic stewardship*?

*See definition on page 10.

Nurturing your faith: Which spiritual practices are best for you?

"Be still, and know that I am God..."

Psalm 46:10

*"You are the salt of the earth; but if salt has lost its taste,
how can its saltiness be restored?..."*

Matthew 5:13

Suggested Group Questions:

Spiritual practices include prayer in its many forms, journaling, creating mandalas, meditation, active imagination exercises, dream work, and walking the labyrinth. Which practices do you prefer?

How do you incorporate spiritual practices into your everyday life?

How has carrying out spiritual practices affected your life?

Which spiritual practices would you like to try?

Group Exploration

Turn to the quotes on the following pages. Read each one slowly. Members of your group may wish to take turns reading them out loud. Pause after reading each one to note any thoughts or emotions. Here are some questions to think about:

Does the quote inspire, surprise, anger, confuse, console, amuse, or leave you cold?

What issues, questions, or concerns does the quote raise?

How does the quote relate to your own personal experiences?

Quotes

There is a wonderful welcome within. Meister Eckhart illuminates this point. He says that there is a place in the soul that neither space nor time nor flesh can touch. This is the eternal place within us. It would be a lovely gift to yourself to go there often—to be nourished, strengthened and renewed.

O'Donohue (1997: p.105)

The self will surely suffer if egotism leads a person away from the experience of the Human Community. And the commonweal as surely suffers if those who wish for its betterment are hollowed-out self-neglecters.

Levertov (1981: p.96)

An important thing to remember is that our own efforts do not produce the God connection. We do not bring God to us by means of something we achieve, as un-American as that sounds. We can only experience the God who is already here. Our efforts, then, are to enhance openness and availability. Spirituality is deepened by access. It is not God who is unavailable. It is you and I.

Ware (1997: pp.2–3)

...much of contemporary spirituality floats in midair. It has no social agenda or conscience, because it is not incarnational. It isn't grounded in community or history. It is too much "big mind" with no "small mind" to fill the gaps.

We need to move toward a contemplation that is socially engaged, tied to the earth. It must have the reach of the big mind, but not be afraid to deal with local exigencies of building a community and addressing questions of oppression.

Rohr (1999: p.109)

(quotes continued on next page)

Quotes *(continued)*

> People come to labyrinths for a multitude of reasons, but most find that walking the labyrinth can be a transformative experience. As people tread through the turns and counterturns of the labyrinth, the world begins to drop away. Walking, breathing, being—things that we never think about in the day-to-day whirl of life—become conscious and deliberate. The spiritual and physical merge into a walking meditation.
>
> **Curry (2000: p.6)**

My Notes

Suggested Reading for Further Exploration

Baldwin, Christina, *Life's Companion: Journal Writing as a Spiritual Quest* (New York: Bantam Books, 1990).

Curry, Helen, *The Way of the Labyrinth: A Powerful Meditation for Everyday Life* (New York: Penguin Compass, 2000).

Erakko Taylor, Barbara, *Silence: Making the Journey to Inner Quiet* (Philadelphia: Innisfree Press, 1997).

Gruff, Kent Ira, *Active Spirituality: A Guide for Seekers and Ministers* (Bethesda, MD: Alban Institute, 1993).

Johnson, Robert A., *Inner Work: Using Dreams & Active Imagination for Personal Growth and Integration* (San Francisco: HarperCollins, 1989).

Kelsey, Morton T., *Dreams: A Way to Listen to God* (New York: Paulist Press, 1978).

Leckey, Dolores R., *Seven Essentials for the Spiritual Journey* (New York: Crossroad Publishing Co., 1999).

Moon, Sharon, *The Healing Oasis: Guided Meditations for Mind, Body and Spirit* (Toronto: United Church Publishing House, 1998).

Morris, Danny E., and Charles M. Olsen, *Discerning God's Will Together: A Spiritual Practice for the Church* (Bethesda, MD: Alban Institute, 1997).

Olsen, Charles M., Ellen Morseth, Jeannie Crawford-Lee, ed., *Selecting Church Leaders: A Practice in Spiritual Discernment* (Nashville: Upper Room Books, 2002).

Thompson, Marjorie J., *Soul Feast: An Invitation to the Christian Spiritual Life* (Louisville, KY: Westminster John Knox Press, 1995).

Tindal, Mardi, *Soul Maps: A Guide to the Midlife Spirit* (Toronto: United Church Publishing House, 2003).

Question 11

What is this community called church?

Meeting Format

Meal

Gathering Time

Opening

Check-in

Spiritual Practices/Prayer:
Praying with Scripture: Matthew 21:12-17

Theme Exploration:
Church

Checkout

Closing

Suggested Praying with Scripture passage: Matthew 21:12-17

Then Jesus entered the temple and drove out all who were selling and buying in the temple, and he overturned the tables of the money changers and the seats of those who sold doves. He said to them, "It is written, 'My house shall be called a house of prayer'; but you are making it a den of robbers."

The blind and the lame came to him in the temple, and he cured them. But when the chief priests and the scribes saw the amazing things that he did, and heard the children crying out in the temple, "Hosanna to the Son of David," they became angry and said to him, "Do you hear what these are saying?" Jesus said to them, "Yes; have you never read, 'Out of the mouths of infants and nursing babies you have prepared praise for yourself'?"

He left them, went out of the city to Bethany, and spent the night there.

See page 155 for information on Praying with Scripture.

Personal Exploration

What words or images, whether positive or challenging, do you associate with the word below? Explore the feelings that they evoke and some of the experiences attached to them.

Church

How has your understanding and experience of church changed over the years?

How have these changes affected the way you live in the world and how you engage in holistic stewardship*?

*See definition on page 10.

What is this community called church?

But we appeal to you, brothers and sisters, to respect those who labor among you, and have charge of you in the Lord and admonish you; esteem them very highly in love because of their work. Be at peace among yourselves.

1 Thessalonians 5:12–13

For just as the body is one and has many members, and all the members of the body, though many, are one body, so it is with Christ. Now you are the body of Christ and individually members of it.

1 Corinthians 12:12, 27

Suggested Group Questions:

Do we need congregations?
How is a congregation different from other gatherings of people, such as social or political groups?
What are some of the positive and not so positive congregational experiences that you have had?
How can we develop congregations that nurture personal and communal growth?

Group Exploration

Turn to the quotes on the following page. Read each one slowly. Members of your group may wish to take turns reading them out loud. Pause after reading each one to note any thoughts or emotions. Here are some questions to think about:

Does the quote inspire, surprise, anger, confuse, console, amuse, or leave you cold?
What issues, questions, or concerns does the quote raise?
How does the quote relate to your own personal experiences?

Quotes

I am deeply aware of my tendency to want to go from communion to ministry without forming community. My individualism and desire for personal success ever and again tempt me to do it alone and claim the task of ministry for myself. But Jesus himself didn't preach and heal alone. Luke the Evangelist tells us how he spent the night in communion with God, the morning to form community with the twelve apostles, and the afternoon to go out with them ministering to the crowds.

Nouwen (1994: p.87)

We are not called to confront oppressive systems alone but as community.

Noe (2001: p.43)

One of the main reasons that a healthy spirituality requires regular church attendance and participation is that, quite simply, we cannot grow and develop on our own. We need to root our spirituality in the richest possible soil so that it will bear fruit.

Langford (2001: p.66)

Clergy and laity often seem anxious and critical as they eye each other's authority. Clergy face new dilemmas about their own authority. The traditional consensus about pastoral authority has collapsed. In the shadow of ecclesiastical academics and bureaucrats, parish pastors often feel they have little authority. On the margin of society, shrinking in numbers, churches themselves wonder what authority they can claim. New wisdom from the human sciences keeps challenging our traditional understanding of what it means to be a leader. As clergy wrestle with their own authority, they are increasingly aware of the central importance of lay people's ministry in the world. Laity face their own dilemmas. Urged to own their ministries at work, at home, and in their communities, they are simultaneously given the message… that clergy, not laity, are the real authorities.

Hahn (1998: p.4)

My Notes

Suggested Reading for Further Exploration

Ackerman, John, *Spiritual Awakening: A Guide to Spiritual Life in Congregations* (Bethesda, MD: Alban Institute, 1994).

Friend, Howard E., *Recovering the Sacred Center: Church Renewal from the Inside Out* (Valley Forge, PA: Judson Press, 1998).

Hahn, Celia Allison, *Growing in Authority: Relinquishing Control: A New Approach to Faithful Leadership* (Bethesda, MD: Alban Institute, 1994).

Hahn, Celia Allison, *Uncovering Your Church's Hidden Spirit* (Bethesda, MD: Alban Institute, 2001).

Hebblethwaite, Margaret, *Basic is Beautiful: Basic Ecclesial Communities from Third World to First World* (London: HarperCollinsPublishers, 1993).

Howard-Brook, Wes, *The Church Before Christianity* (Maryknoll, NY: Orbis Books, 2001).

Morrill, Bruce T., Bernard J. Cooke, eds., *Bodies of Worship: Explorations in Theory and Practice* (Collegeville, MN: Liturgical Press, 2000).

Morris, Danny E., and Charles M. Olsen, *Discerning God's Will Together: A Spiritual Practice for the Church* (Bethesda, MD: Alban Institute, 1997).

Olsen, Charles M., *Transforming Church Boards into Communities of Spiritual Leaders* (Boulder, CO: netLibrary, 1995).

Olsen, Charles M., Ellen Morseth, Jeannie Crawford-Lee, eds., *Selecting Church Leaders: A Practice in Spiritual Discernment* (Nashville: Upper Room Books, 2002).

Stairs, Jean, *Listening for the Soul: Pastoral Care and Spiritual Direction* (Minneapolis: Fortress Press, 2003).

Ware, Corinne, *Connecting to God: Nurturing Spirituality Through Small Groups* (Bethesda, MD: Alban Institute, 1997).

Question 12

How do you live your faith in the world?

Meeting Format

Meal

Gathering Time

Opening

Check-in

Spiritual Practices/Prayer:
Praying with Scripture: Matthew 22:36-40

Theme Exploration:
Living Your Faith in the World

Checkout

Closing

Suggested Praying with Scripture passage: Matthew 22:36-40

"Teacher, which commandment in the law is the greatest?"

He said to him, " 'You shall love the Lord your God with all your heart, and with all your soul, and with all your mind.' This is the greatest and first commandment. And a second is like it: 'You shall love your neighbor as yourself.' On these two commandments hang all the law and the prophets."

See page 155 for information on Praying with Scripture.

Personal Exploration

What words or images, whether positive or challenging, do you associate with the phrase below? Explore the feelings that they evoke and some of the experiences attached to them.

Living Your Faith in the World

How has your understanding and experience of living your faith in the world changed over the years?

How have these changes affected the way you live in the world and how you engage in holistic stewardship*?

*See definition on page 10.

How do you live your faith in the world?

...and what does the Lord require of you but to do justice,
and to love kindness, and to walk humbly with your God?

Micah 6:8

...if we love one another, God lives in us,
and [God's] love is perfected in us.

1 John 4:12

Suggested Group Questions:

How does your faith affect the way you live in the world?
What challenges does the world pose to your faith?
What challenges does your faith pose to the world?
How does your congregation live out its faith in the world?
How does your congregation resist living out its faith in the world?

Group Exploration

Turn to the quotes on the following pages. Read each one slowly. Members of your group may wish to take turns reading them out loud. Pause after reading each one to note any thoughts or emotions. Here are some questions to think about:

Does the quote inspire, surprise, anger, confuse, console, amuse, or leave you cold?
What issues, questions, or concerns does the quote raise?
How does the quote relate to your own personal experiences?

Quotes

Those of us claiming to follow Jesus are called to be with those who Jesus was with, those who are on the margins or not even on the system's map at all and those relationships will always lead to the confrontation of unjust systems.

Noe (2001: p.42)

Being with the suffering and excluded in ways that are healing and empowering requires entering their presence with an understanding that we do not bring God to others, but that God is already in them. Our hope is that through God's grace we might re-kindle and fan the flame of Divine Love in each other.

Noe (2001: p.37)

The mission is always first of all to our own, our family, our friends, those who are an intimate part of our lives. This is not a very comfortable realization. I always find it harder to speak about Jesus to those who know me intimately than to those who have never had to deal with my "peculiar ways of being." Still there lies a great challenge here. Somehow the authenticity of our experience is tested by our parents, our spouses, our children, our brothers and sisters, all those who know us all too well.

Nouwen (1994: p.82)

Any religion which professes to be concerned about the souls of [people] and is not concerned about the social and economic conditions that can scar the soul, is a spiritually moribund religion only waiting for the day to be buried.

King, Jr. (1958: p.72)

(quotes continued on next page)

Quotes *(continued)*

The Power of the Christian Community

Because money talks
But rarely conceives
Because money talks
But does not walk
We call upon Your name
Because there are things
money can't buy
because what does it profit us
    if we consume the whole world
    and are consumed in the process
    because we are tired
    of being paralysed
    in pain and guilt and powerlessness.

We call upon Your name
when we have neither silver nor gold
or when we have it all
and it means nothing.
We call upon the Power
of Your name, Your Power
between us and among us.

to ourselves, sick and lame
by the gate—
Rise. Walk.
Sing Justice. Sow Glory.

Anderson (1993: pp.117–118)

My Notes

Suggested Reading for Further Exploration

Brooke, Avery, *Healing in the Landscape of Prayer* (Cambridge, MA: Cowley Publications, 2002).

Dossey, Larry, *Healing Through Prayer: Health Practitioners Tell The Story* (Toronto: Anglican Book Centre, 1999).

Hall, Douglas J., *Professing the Faith: Christian Theology in a North American Context* (Minneapolis, MN: Fortress Press, 2003).

Leddy, Mary Jo, *Radical Gratitude* (Maryknoll, NY: Orbis Books, 2002).

Noe, K. Killian, *Finding Our Way Home: Addictions and Divine Love* (Scottsdale, PA: Herald Press, 2003).

Palmer, Parker J., *The Company of Strangers: Christians and the Renewal of America's Public Life* (New York: Crossroad Publishing, 1983).

Shore, Edith, *Lying Down with Lions: Building the Peaceable Kingdom—Helping Women Who Have Served Time in Prison and Building Healthy Communities* (Toronto: Inter-Church Working Group on Violence and Sexual Abuse c/o The United Church of Canada, 2000).

Question 13

The journey continues, what is next?

Meeting Format

Meal

Gathering Time

Opening

Check-in

Spiritual Practices/Prayer:
Praying with Scripture: Matthew 28:16-20

Theme Exploration:
Personal Faith Journey

Checkout

Closing

Suggested Praying with Scripture passage: Matthew 28:16-20

Now the eleven disciples went to Galilee, to the mountain to which Jesus had directed them. When they saw him, they worshiped him; but some doubted. And Jesus came and said to them, "All authority in heaven and on earth has been given to me. Go therefore and make disciples of all nations, baptizing them in the name of [God] and of the Son and of the Holy Spirit, and teaching them to obey everything that I have commanded you. And remember, I am with you always, to the end of the age."

See page 155 for information on Praying with Scripture.

Personal Exploration

What words or images, whether positive or challenging, do you associate with the phrase below? Explore the feelings that they evoke and some of the experiences attached to them.

How has your understanding and experience of your personal faith journey changed over the past few weeks?

How have these changes affected the way you live in the world and how you engage in holistic stewardship*?

*See definition on page 10.

The journey continues, what is next?

O give thanks to the God of heaven,
for God's steadfast love endures forever.

Psalm 136:26

As they came near the village to which they were going,
he walked ahead as if he were going on.
But they urged him strongly, saying, "Stay with us, because it is almost evening
and the day is now nearly over." So he went in to stay with them.

Luke 24:28–29

Suggested Group Questions:

For what do you feel gratitude as you come to an end of these meetings?
For what do you feel regret?
Has your personal faith journey shifted in some way over the past few weeks? If so, how?
What session was particularly important to you? Why?
What theme or themes would you like to explore further?

Group Exploration

Turn to the quotes on the following page. Read each one slowly. Members of your group may wish to take turns reading them out loud. Pause after reading each one to note any thoughts or emotions. Here are some questions to think about:

Does the quote inspire, surprise, anger, confuse, console, amuse, or leave you cold?
What issues, questions, or concerns does the quote raise?
How does the quote relate to your own personal experiences?

Quotes

The more you are called to speak for God's love, the more you will need to deepen the knowledge of that love in your own heart. The farther the outward journey takes you, the deeper the inner journey must be.

Nouwen (1996: pp.93–4)

We shall not cease from exploration
And the end of all our exploring
Will be to arrive where we started
And to know the place for the first time.

Eliot (1974: p.58)

If we live in God, we will find ourselves on pilgrimage; we will be taken to alien places where we are strangers and estranged. Only when we acknowledge that "you can't go home again" will we be on the road to faith.

Palmer (1999: p.63)

My Notes

Suggested Reading for Further Exploration

Knitter, Paul F., *Introducing Theologies of Religions* (Maryknoll, NY: Orbis Books, 2002).

McFague, Sallie, *Life Abundant: Rethinking Theology and Economy for a Planet in Peril* (Minneapolis, MN: Fortress Press, 2003).

Pohl, Christine D., *Making Room: Recovering Hospitality as a Christian Tradition* (Grand Rapids, MI: Eerdmans William B. Publishing Company, 1999).

Ramey Mollenkott, Virginia, *Omnigender: A Trans-Religious Approach* (Cleveland, Ohio: Pilgrim Press, The United Church Press, 2001).

Rieger, Joerg, *God and the Excluded; Visions and Blindspots in Contemporary Theology* (Minneapolis, MN: Fortress Press, 2003).

Snyder, Mary Hembrow, ed., *Spiritual Questions for the Twenty-First Century: Essays in Honor of Joan Chittister* (Maryknoll, NY: Orbis Books, 2001).

Vest, Norvene, *Still Listening: New Horizons in Spiritual Direction* (Harrisburg, PA: Morehouse Publishing, 2000).

Ware, Corinne, *Discover Your Spiritual Type: A Guide to Individual and Congregational Growth* (Bethesda, MD: Alban Institute, 1995).

Appendix A

Notes for the Facilitator

Starting Exploring Faith Questions *Covenant Groups*

Exploring Faith Questions groups are encouraged to meet as covenant groups. Covenant groups are small groups that meet for an agreed upon length of time for a specific purpose. Group participants create a covenant based on what they need to feel safe and participate as fully as possible, and the norms and values they wish to uphold as a group. Groups usually develop the covenant during the second session. (See sample covenant below)

Getting *Exploring Faith Questions* groups going in a congregation can happen in a variety of ways. They may be formally organized. For example, someone in the congregation may advertise times and length of covenant groups, find facilitators, and spaces for the groups to meet, consider meal options, and organize the participants into groups.

Groups can also be organized less formally. For example, a group of interested people may decide to form their own group and seek out a facilitator to work with them. Or someone interested in facilitating a group may bring together a group of women and men that he or she knows or get the word out that a group is forming and see if enough people show interest to start a group.

Early on in the process of bringing a group together, usually but not necessarily before the first meeting, the following information will be available for participants:

- where and when the group will meet
- how many meetings there will be, that is, the length of the covenant period
- how long the meetings will be
- who will facilitate
- if the meeting time will include a meal
- how to share meal and perhaps other responsibilities

Who Facilitates?

Exploring Faith Questions stresses personal experience and not arriving at a particular theological position. The facilitator, therefore, does not need to have a depth of knowledge about all the faith questions, nor is she or he expected to have the last word on any of the questions. The facilitator, however, needs to be able to create a "safe" atmosphere for the group so that participants feel comfortable talking about their experiences. Since *Exploring Faith Questions* also stresses spiritual formation as part of the group experience, the facilitator should be comfortable leading prayer and be open to the leadings of the spirit.

A group may decide to have two facilitators. Facilitators could share the responsibilities of leading the group from session to session, or one may wish to take on a specific role, such as leading the spiritual practice.

The Meeting

The Meal (½-1 hour)

Groups are encouraged to begin their meeting with a meal, to break bread together. Some groups may decide to have a meal meeting at each meeting or just for a couple of them. Once participants decide where they will meet – at each other's homes or at the church – they decide the format the meal will take.

Gathering Time (15-20 min. prior to the scheduled meeting time.)

A time for informal socializing before the meeting begins. Care should be taken that the meeting starts on time. Groups that are having a meal together before the meeting would not need a formal gathering time. Groups that have a meal meeting may, however, need to have a brief transition time between the meal and the rest of the meeting.

Opening (2-5 min.)

The opening is a time of quieting, of stilling, a time of bringing the group together. This opening time could include a brief prayer followed or preceded by a ritual, poem, or a song. It is also a time to establish a ritual (e.g. lighting a candle) with which the group comes to identify as its own.

Check-in (30 min.)

Check-in is a time for each participant to share personally and for the rest of the group to listen attentively. For the check-in the facilitator invites each participant to reflect upon a question. The question could be as simple as, "How are you this evening?"

No matter what check-in approach is used this is not a discussion time. "Cross talk" should be avoided. Each participant talks without comment from the rest. If necessary, a clarifying question may be asked. There should not be any judgmental comments—good or bad.

Prayer/Spiritual Practices (30 min.)

Groups are encouraged to do Praying with Scripture as its spiritual practice. This practice helps to create community based on respectful listening and prayerful intention.
(See Appendix B.)

Exploring a Faith Question (60-75 min.)

1. Personal Exploration

A process for participants to explore the questions is provided on page 9. Participants are encouraged to do some personal work before each meeting. The exercise is useful but not mandatory. Not having done the personal exploration will not in any way hinder participation in the group discussion. Having done the exercise will make the experience richer. Facilitators are encouraged to do their own personal work as well.

Encourage participants to do their personal exploration ***before*** they read the biblical texts or quotes. This allows participants to begin their exploration of the faith question with their own experiences rather than responding or reacting to other material.

If participants find it difficult to find the time to do this exercise prior to the meeting but still want to do it, facilitators might suggest taking the first 10 minutes or so of this part of the meeting to complete the exercise.

2. General discussion of the faith question

The facilitator has to help the group find ways to approach the question that encourage open, thoughtful and respectful participation. Basic guidelines for discussion such as the following can be included in the covenant:

- One person speaks at a time
- Always speak from your own experience
- All experiences are valid and respected

- Comments that put down, belittle or dismiss yourself or others are not acceptable
- Speak only for yourself; let others speak for themselves
- Use "I" statements to express emotions, e.g., "I feel angry when you say that." rather than, "You make me feel angry."
- No one is "right" and has the privilege to force her or his views on others. All participants should have the opportunity to express their views, and hear those of others.

Tools for Discussion

A couple of biblical passages and a few non-biblical quotes are included for each question. A few questions have also been included for each faith question to help promote and deepen discussion. Facilitators are encouraged to develop their own.

Beginning the Discussion

The facilitator may want to begin by reading the quotes and ask for response, move on to the quotes, and then raise some of the suggested questions when appropriate.

Another way to begin the discussion would be to have each participant state in a word or at very most a phrase, how they feel or what they think about the question. After this initial response you could then move on to the scripture passages or the quotes, raise a question related to something someone has said, or ask a participant to expand on her or his comment.

Keeping the Discussion Going

Given the nature of the material keeping the discussion going should not be difficult. If discussion does stop, go back to one of the scripture passages, quotes or questions and ask for example, "In light of what we've heard, how would you respond to this now?"

If the group goes off topic, the facilitator may wish to use a scripture passage, quote or question to bring the group back on track. The facilitator and the group as a whole need to keep in mind that there is not material that *must* be covered. Nevertheless, participants have joined the group to discuss faith questions. If it looks like the group is becoming a different type of discussion group, the covenant should be revisited and if necessary changed.

Keeping the Discussion Civil

Differing views arising from differing personal experience are inevitable. Having different views is not a problem. How the group deals with the differences can be a challenge. Since the purpose of *Exploring Faith Questions* is to allow participants the opportunity to explore openly and honestly out of their own experiences and not to have to come to and to adhere to a particular theological position, it is very important that the opportunity be created for this to happen. Keeping a prayerful, compassionate space is imperative.

This is particularly challenging for the facilitator who must be able to encourage honest discussion and consequently risk conflict. This is very different from provoking conflict for the sake of conflict, which should be avoided. Nevertheless, when conflict arises, it needs to be honoured. It must not be dismissed for fear of dealing with it. The experiences and views of one or more of the participants are not to be diminished or belittled if they do not coincide with those of the rest of the group. Facilitators must be able to help participants respect each other's views.

If participants start to become angry or upset, the facilitator may suggest, for example, that the group take a few minutes in silence to reflect on what's been said. After a minute or two the facilitator asks participants to say in a word or a phrase where they stand on the question. For example, in a discussion of "Who is Jesus for you" the participants' different understandings of Jesus are making some of the participants defensive and others angry. In this case the facilitator may ask the basic faith question, "Who is Jesus for you?" Michelle might say "a personal saviour," Ian could consider Jesus "a prophet," Jack understands Jesus as "a friend, a companion on the way," and Margo replies, "a teacher and a healer."

What is important is that the participants hear the differences while owning their own positions and respecting those of others. If the group focuses on experience rather than on opinion, differences can be discussed more easily. For example, the questions can then be asked: Michelle, how do you experience Jesus as a personal saviour? Ian, how do you experience Jesus as a prophet? Jack, how do you experience Jesus as a friend? Margo, how do you experience Jesus as a teacher and healer?

If the discussion starts to become bitter, you might take a moment and offer what you have been hearing to God in prayer. Just offer the group to God without judgment before continuing the discussion. You also may have to revisit the covenant to remind participants of the discussion guidelines and add new ones if necessary.

Reflection Time

Toward the end of the discussion time the facilitator may wish to have the participants take a couple of minutes to reflect on what they have been hearing, thinking and feeling. This can lead into the check-out.

Check-out (5-10 min.)

A *brief* time for each participant to reflect on what has happened in the group session especially with regard to any insights that may affect the participants' day-to-day lives. The insights may relate directly to the faith question explored or perhaps to something experienced during another part of the meeting, for example, the check-in or prayer time.

To keep this part of the meeting from becoming too long, participants may, for example, be asked to think of a word, or an image arising from the meeting that is meaningful to them and then to connect it with an image or event that is related to their day-to-day life. A primary question here may be, Where is your faith leading you in your relationship with others—family, friends, colleagues, even strangers?

The facilitator may also ask participants to write down the word, phrase, or sentence, or draw the image that best answers one or more of the following:

- How do you feel after this time together?
- Have you gained a particular insight during this group time?
- Has a significant question or concern been raised for you?
- How does what you have heard or experienced during the meeting relate to some aspect of your personal life?

Participants may wish to use the "My Notes" page for this exercise and share some of this briefly with the group. This form of journaling may also be helpful to participants during the time between sessions.

Closing (2-5 min.)

A brief prayer followed or preceded by a ritual, poem, or a song. The closing is a time to bring the group back together as a unit and to bring closure to the session.

Sample Introductory Meeting

Beginning the Journey

The introductory session, **Beginning the Journey**, introduces participants to the series *Exploring Faith Questions*. During this session participants follow the basic small group meeting format: meal, opening, check-in, spiritual practices, discussion time, check-out, and closing.

Meal: For the introductory meeting, the facilitator may wish to organize the meal. During the meeting participants can decide how the rest will be done.

Opening: Choose something simple that helps participants to centre.

Check-in: Choose a question that helps participants get to know each other but that is not overly personal or puts people unnecessarily on the spot.

Spiritual practices: For a passage suggestion for Praying with Scripture see Appendix B. Whoever leads the practice should have reviewed the process before the meeting.

Discussion time: The group:

- Confirms which questions they wish to explore.
- Participants will probably already be expecting to covenant for a particular number of weeks, perhaps six or eight, but the faith questions that they will discuss may possibly be worked out at this initial meeting.
- Discusses what it means to be a covenant group.

  Facilitator reviews what it means to be part of a covenant group, distributes information regarding covenant groups and a sample covenant to be completed during the second meeting. Once the covenant is complete copies should be given to all participants.Spends time talking about spiritual practices. Participants discuss how they wish to carry out this part of the meeting. There are many possibilities. The group may wish to do praying with scripture for the whole covenant period or use this practice for a couple of weeks. It may also wish to have a guided meditation for a couple of weeks, do some contemplative prayer or use other practices.

Check-out: It is recommended that the group begin to do some journaling as part of the check-out process. Keep it simple. The facilitator might want to ask participants to write down a word or to draw an image that comes to mind as they are finishing their first meeting together.

Closing: Again, keep it very simple for the first meeting.

Exploring Faith Questions

Sample Covenant

Participants:

Meeting time:

Meeting day:

Meeting place:

Facilitator(s):

What do participants need to feel safe and participate as fully as possible?

What norms and values do we wish to uphold as a group?

Appendix B

Spiritual Practices for Small Groups

Praying with Scripture

(also referred to as African Bible Reflection, African Model, or Lambeth Method)

Praying with Scripture is a very effective spiritual exercise for groups. Through this exercise, we will learn to:

- listen more deeply to the scriptures
- voice our own personal struggles with God's call
- listen prayerfully and attentively to others
- be comfortable with silence
- pray for one another
- respect our own and others' experiences of and responses to scripture
- keep confidences
- accompany one another on our faith journeys

Here are three important principles of this method:

- What is said in the group stays in the group. Strict confidentiality is to be observed.
- Participants may pass if they do not wish to respond or cannot think of anything to say.
- While one person is speaking, the others listen without responding at all. There is NO discussion.

The facilitator will explain the nature of the exercise:

- This is a reflection based on personal experience and not a historical or theological study of the text.
- The scripture text will be read three times (the same version or different versions), by three different people throughout the exercise.

- A period of deep silence follows each reading.
- What is shared in the group remains in the group.
- Participants may pass and may decide not to share verbally.
- Each person's reflections should be listened to and not commented upon by others.

Praying with Scripture: The Process

Part 1

The facilitator tells group members to listen for a word or phrase that catches their attention.

The facilitator asks someone to read the passage out loud while everyone else listens without looking at the text. (The reader puts the text away.)

Silence follows for at least one minute.

The facilitator asks the participants to recall a word or phrase that came to mind during the period of silence and share it with the group. There is no further explanation or discussion. (Participants should never feel apologetic about what they say.)

Part 2

In preparation for the second reading of the passage, the facilitator asks the group to listen for how the passage is speaking to their lives today.

The facilitator asks a second person to read while the other participants listen. (The reader puts the text away.)

Silence follows for at least three minutes as the participants listen to where the passage is connecting with some part of their lives, whether personal, work, or congregational.

Participants share their responses without any discussion.

Part 3

In preparation for the third reading of the passage, the facilitator asks the group to listen to it for the last time and consider the following questions: "From what I have heard and shared, how does God want me to be? What does God want me to do or be this week? How does God want me to change?"

The facilitator also tells the group that after the sharing time, each person will be asked to pray for the person to his or her left, in response to what that person shared.

The passage is read by a third person while the others listen. (The reader puts the text away.)

Silence follows for three to five minutes as participants listen to the way the passage is speaking to them in terms of being, acting, or changing.

Participants share their responses.

Participants join hands and take turns praying for the person to their left.

Pray around the circle, going to the right. (The one who starts prays for the person on his or her left, then the person on his or her right prays next and so on. This may seem confusing and unnecessary, but it means that the person who is praying has not just been prayed for. Receiving prayer can be an emotional experience.)

Participants conclude the session by saying the Lord's Prayer together.

Suggested Passages for Praying with Scripture

Introductory Meeting: Beginning the Journey, Considering the Questions (Luke 18:35–43)

Question 1: Faith: What is it? How can we talk about it? (Psalm 139:1–6)

Question 2: How do you experience God in your life? (Acts 17:22–28)

Question 3: Who is Jesus for you? (Matthew 15:21–28)

Question 4: The Bible: What does it mean to you? (Matthew 12:1–8)

Question 5: Prayer: What does it mean to you? (Luke 11:9–13)

Question 6: How can we talk about God and suffering? (Luke 13:10–17)

Question 7: Who me, a sinner? (Luke 18:9–14)

Question 8: Forgiveness: What are the challenges and the blessings? (Luke 5:27–32)

Question 9: After death: What is next? (1 Corinthians 13:8–13)

Question 10: Nurturing your faith: Which spiritual practices are best for you? (Matthew 6:1–8)

Question 11: What is this community called church? (Matthew 21:12–17)

Question 12: How do we live our faith in the world? (Matthew 22:36–40)

Question 13: The journey continues, what is next? (Matthew 28:16–20)

Centring Prayer

If the group is new or if there are newcomers, the facilitator briefly explains the guidelines for centring prayer:

- Choose a sacred word as the symbol of your intention to consent to God's presence and action within, for example, love, shalom, abba, om, peace. This is a personal choice and may be changed from one prayer time to the next, but should be kept during any given prayer session.
- Sitting comfortably, with your eyes closed and back straight, settle briefly and silently introduce the sacred word as the symbol of your consent to God's presence and action within.
- When you become aware of your thoughts, gently return to the sacred word.
- At the end of the prayer time, remain in silence, with your eyes closed, for a few minutes.

Before beginning the prayer time, encourage participants to find a comfortable place: sitting in a chair, sitting on the floor, or leaning against the wall. Participants should try to keep their backs as straight as possible.

It is necessary to mark the beginning and end of the prayer time using chimes, a bell, a singing bowl, or taped meditation music. The advantage of using a meditation tape is that the facilitator can easily participate in the prayer time without thinking about marking the end of the session. You may purchase meditation tapes or make your own by recording an appropriate piece of music onto an audio cassette, leaving a period of silence of about five to 30 minutes, and recording the music again. The point at which the music begins again indicates that the centring prayer time is coming to an end. You may wish to begin with five minutes of silence and gradually increase the silence to 20 or 30 minutes.

Additional Prayer Practices for Small Groups

Encountering God in Everyday Objects

Choose any object: a stone, a leaf, something from the kitchen, a tool, or a picture. Remember that everything is a source of prayer and conversation with God, who is near and present in the ordinary.

Hold the object in your hand and look closely at it. What does it feel like? What do you see? What colour is the object? What do you like about it?

What does your object tell you about yourself? Are you like this object in any way? Who does this object remind you of? Which place in this world does the object remind you of? Does your object tell you something about God? How is God like this object?

Enter your heart or special place in your imagination, where you can talk with God using the object as a theme for the prayer. What would you like to say to God at this moment? What is the most loving thing God might say to you? Listen silently.

End this activity by thanking God for surrounding us and being present in all things.

Holding What Gives Us Life...

Sleeping with Bread: Holding What Gives You Life by Dennis Linn, Sheila Fabricant Linn, and Matthew Linn (New York: Paulist Press) 1995.

This book tells a story about children who experienced the bombing raids of World War II, particularly of those who were left orphaned and hungry. While living in the refugee camps, they were so frightened that they were unable to sleep. Someone thought of giving each child a piece of bread before they went to bed. Holding this piece of bread helped the children to sleep. They slept peacefully, knowing there would be bread for the next day. Throughout the night, the bread reminded them that: "Today I ate, and I will eat again tomorrow."

The book suggests the following ritual for the end of the day:

> Light a candle and ask yourself:
> For what moment today am I most grateful?
>   (*silent meditation*)
> For what moment today am I least grateful?
>   (*silent meditation*)

Listening Exercise

Sit in your chair, upright but comfortably, with your back supported.

Notice the sounds you can hear, sounds far away. Just hear them without trying to name them.

Notice fainter sounds, then sounds that are nearer. Just listen and become aware of them.

And the sound of your own heartbeat, faint, your own rhythm of life...

And the sound of silence in your place of prayer, the silence within yourself.

Listen like this for a few minutes.

Sacred Space

Pause for a few minutes and to take some sacred space. Take some deep, refreshing breaths. Remember that in the midst of this day (or night) you are in the presence of God. Ponder these words: *"Be still, and know that I am God!..."* (Psalm 46:10)

Allow the words to begin to fit the rhythm of your breathing: "Be still, and know" as you breathe in and "that I am God!" as you breathe out.

As you take this quiet space to pray and reflect, you join in an unceasing rhythm of prayer going on all around the world. And, in the words of the poet, "More things are wrought by prayer than this world dreams of." Prayer makes a difference.

What is the deepest prayer of your heart right now? Allow it to be heard. Remember that Jesus often said to people, "What do you want me to do for you?" Hear your prayer into being. Take your time. It is your time, your sacred space.

When you are ready to leave this sacred space, offer a prayer for at least one other person, community, local, national, or world situation.

Appendix C

Give Your Undergarment Too

The first paragraph of this commentary appeared as a quote for the Question 8 "Forgiveness: What are the challenges and the blessings?" Here is the rest of the commentary.

If you do as the passage [Matthew 5:38–41] says and turn your other cheek (your left cheek) and your master must use his right hand [the left is for unclean tasks], then he can no longer backhand you [a gesture used to humiliate another]. If he hits you again, he will have to use his fist. Hitting another with a fist was a gesture used only between equals. Thus, by turning your other cheek, you have reclaimed your dignity and communicated that you refuse to be humiliated. You have also invited your master to reclaim his true dignity by examining the lie by which he lives, that one human being is better than another. And you have done all this non-violently, without striking back.

The next part of the passage says, "...and if anyone wants to sue you and take your coat, give your cloak as well." The context of this passage is a highly exploitive economic system, in which wealthy landowners charged high interest rates for loans, forcing poor people into defaulting and losing their land. For those who had already lost everything, the only collateral they had left was their "*himation*" (translated here as "coat" and meaning outer garment).

The scene unfolds in a courtroom, and you, a poor person, are being asked to turn over your outer garment as collateral. Your creditor is literally taking the "shirt off your back." Jesus says, "Give your '*chiton*' (translated here as "cloak" and meaning undergarment*) as well." In Jesus' culture, a chiton might be worn by itself without embarrassment. However,

* In this passage from Matthew, it is actually the *chiton*, rather than the *himation*, that is demanded. However, in the parallel passage in Luke 6:29–30 the order is reversed so that what is demanded is the *himation*. The Jewish practice of giving the outer garment as collateral, referred to in Exodus 22:25–27, makes it evident that Luke's order is correct.

since nothing was worn underneath it, giving it away would be as if, in our culture, you gave away your underwear. Whether you give away your underwear in our culture or if you gave away your chiton in Jesus' culture, you would be naked. In Jesus' culture, it was not as improper to be naked yourself as it was to look at another person who was naked. Your creditor, now in this very situation, must experience the humiliation he has tried to bring upon you. As Walter Wink says, "The creditor is revealed to be not a legitimate moneylender but a party to the reduction of an entire social class to landlessness, destitution, and debasement. This unmasking is not simply punitive, therefore it offers the creditor a chance to see, perhaps for the first time in his life, what his practices cause, and to repent."

You have regained your dignity by taking back your power to choose your own response, all without violence. Moreover, you have offered your oppressor an opportunity for conversion.

Go a Second Mile

The passage continues: "if anyone forces you to go one mile, go also the second mile." In Palestine in the time of Jesus, Roman occupying soldiers could require the local inhabitants to carry their packs. The packs were quite heavy and Roman subjects resented this practice of forced labour. The Romans, who wanted to avoid riots, passed laws limiting the amount of forced labour required. A Roman soldier could force a local civilian to carry a pack only one mile. If the solder demanded more, he himself could be punished.

Imagine that you are a Palestinian local and a Roman soldier demands that you carry his pack. You know how far a mile is because the Roman roads were marked at each mile. You come to the mile marker and, instead of stopping, you continue to carry the pack, without protest. You have confused the Roman solder and he is concerned that he will be punished. Imagine him pleading with you to give him back his pack. Once again you have regained your dignity by exercising your power to choose your own response and refusing to behave as a victim, all without striking the soldier or resorting to violence.

Let's return then to verse 39a: "Do not resist an evildoer." The word that we translate as "resist" is "*antistenai*" in Greek. It means to resist *violently*, to rise up in a military sense. Thus, Jesus is telling us not to take an eye for an eye, not to hit back or return violence in kind. Instead, when someone tries to abuse or humiliate us, Jesus invites us to find a creative, non-violent way to resist and therefore regain our dignity. Even in situations of injustice that we cannot fully change, we can attempt to maintain our power to choose our response instead of remaining passive victims. As Gandhi said, "The first principle of non-violent action is that of non-cooperation with anything humiliating."

—Linn, Dennis, Sheila Fabricant Linn, & Matthew Linn, *Don't Forgive Too Soon: Extending the Two Hands that Heal* (New York: Paulist Press, 1997, pp.5–8).

Appendix D

The United Church of Canada Who We Are and What We Believe

The United Church of Canada, like almost every Christian church, has a statement or statements of its fundamental beliefs. These are often called articles of religion or articles of doctrine. (The word "doctrine" simply means "teaching.") These historic statements have a unique defining role in the faith of the church. At the same time their authority is not unlimited. From the beginning, those who envisioned the United Church believed that Christians could distinguish between "the substance of the faith" and all particular (e.g. denominationally or culturally specific) expressions of it.

For our forebearers, this meant that there would be an ongoing clarification of this substance through periodic restatement, given changing context and challenges. Successive generations in the church have shared this outlook on the ongoing task of restatement. Thus in 1940 the 9th General Council adopted "A Statement of Faith," and in 1968 the 23rd General Council adopted "A New Creed." Currently the Committee on Theology and Faith is beginning work on the draft of "a timely and contextual statement of faith," as mandated by the 37th General Council.

Below follows the most recent interpretation of the ongoing task of restating the faith, as expressed by the November 1997 meeting of the Executive of General Council:

Three words are helpful in clarifying the place of doctrinal standards in The United Church: continuity, context, and diversity.

1) Continuity

The doctrine of The United Church of Canada is set forth in two basic documents, the Basis of Union (1925) and the Statement of Faith (1940). As well, "A New Creed" (1968) is an affirmation of faith used widely in our worship. These standards are authorized by General Councils and belong uniquely to the unfolding life of the United Church. Yet we do not seek to stand alone. As members of one body of Christ, we acknowledge our Reformation heritage and the teaching of the creeds of the ancient church (particularly the Apostles' and Nicene Creeds). Our membership in the World Council of Churches today links us to a fellowship of churches "which confess the Lord Jesus Christ as God and Saviour according to the scriptures." Above all, we trace our continuity in faith to the scriptures of the Old and New Testament, whose witness is the ultimate standard for Christian faith and life.

2) *Context*

The Statement of Faith of 1940 reminds us that "the Church's faith is the unchanging Gospel of God's holy, redeeming love in Jesus Christ." It also declares that each new generation is called to state this gospel afresh, "in terms of the thought of their own age and with the emphasis their age needs." The call to renew our confession has led us not only to the Statement of 1940, but also to "A New Creed" and to other statements such as "The Lordship of Jesus" (1978) and "The Authority and Interpretation of Scripture" (1992). No single statement or creed can capture all that may be required of the church to make the good confession in a new context. Our claim that "Jesus is Lord" must be a timely one. The journey of a pilgrim people goes on.

3) *Diversity*

Based on the understanding that the Bible is the ultimate standard for our faith, the creeds and confessions formulated by the church can only possess a "subordinate authority." Thus, membership in the church is based on a profession of faith and not on a credal subscription or test. New members are asked to profess their faith in the triune God and to commit themselves to faithful conduct in church and world. What is required additionally of those being ordained or commissioned in the United Church is "essential agreement" with the doctrinal articles of the Basis of Union.

We have doctrinal standards and attempt to set them forth in continuity with the biblical faith. But our grasp on the truth of God is finite and fallible, and we do not believe that faithfulness consists in assenting to particular statements. Rarely, if ever, do we use doctrinal standards to exclude anyone from the circle of belonging. Rather we lift up Jesus Christ and his way, saying to all who seek God's grace and service, "Come and see."

References

This section lists the references for the material used in the "Quotes" pages of each chapter. Care has been taken to seek permission to use copyright material contained in this book.

Anderson, Terry A., *Den of Lions: Memoirs of Seven Years* (New York: Janklow/Nesbit Agency, 1993).

Borg, Marcus, *Reading the Bible Again for the First Time: Taking the Bible Seriously But Not Literally* (New York: HarperCollins Publishers, 2002).

Campbell, Joseph, and Fraser Boa, *This Business of the Gods* (Windrose Films Ltd., 1989).

Carse, James P., *The Silence of God: Meditations on Prayer* (Scarborough: HarperCollins Publishers Canada, 1995).

Chittister, Joan, *Living Well: Scriptural Reflections for Every Day* (Maryknoll, NY: Orbis, 2000).

Chittister, Joan, *Scarred by Struggle, Transformed by Hope* (Grand Rapids, MI.: William B. Eerdmans, 2003).

Curry, Helen, *The Way of the Labyrinth: A Powerful Meditation for Everyday Life* (New York: Penguin Compass, 2000).

Daly, Mary, *Beyond God the Father: Toward a Philosophy of Women's Liberation*, 2nd ed. (Boston: Beacon Press, 1993).

de la Torre, Miguel A., *Reading the Bible from the Margins* (Maryknoll, NY: Orbis Books, 2002).

Eliot, T.S, "Little Gidding," in *Four Quartets* (London: Faber & Faber, Inc., 1974).

Fox, Matthew, *Original Blessing: A Primer in Creation Spirituality* (New York: Putnam Publishing Group, 2000).

Gilkey, Langdon, "God," in *Christian Theology: An Introduction to Its Traditions and Tasks*, Peter C. Hodgson and Robert H. King, eds. (Minneapolis, MN: Fortress Press, 2003), pp. 59-90.

Grey, Mary, *Feminism, Redemption and the Christian Tradition* (Mystic, CT: Twenty-Third Publications, 1990).

Hahn, Celia Allison, *Growing in Authority, Relinquishing Control: A New Approach to Faithful Leadership* (Bethesda, MD: Alban Institute, 1994).

Harpur, Tom, *Life After Death* (Toronto: McClelland & Stewart, 1992).

Harpur, Tom, *Would You Believe?: Finding God Without Losing Your Mind* (Toronto: McClelland & Stewart, 1996).

Harpur, Tom, *The Pagan Christ: Rediscovering the Lost Light* (Toronto: Thomas Allen Publishers, 2004).

Heyward, Carter, *Our Passion for Justice: Images of Power, Sexuality, and Liberation* (Cleveland, OH: Pilgrim Press, The United Church Press, 1984), 124. © 1984 The Pilgrim Press. Adapted by permission.

Heyward, Carter, *Saving Jesus From Those Who Are Right* (Minneapolis: Fortress Press, 1999).

Jenco, Lawrence Martin, *Bound to Forgive: The Pilgrimage to Reconciliation of a Beirut Hostage* (Notre Dame, IN: Ave Maria Press, 1995).

Keating, Thomas, *Open Mind, Open Heart: The Contemplative Dimension of the Gospel* (New York: Continuum Press, 1997). Reprinted by permission of The Continuum Publishing Group.

King, Jr., Martin Luther, *Strive Toward Freedom: The Montgomery Story* (New York: Harper & Row, 1958). Copyright renewed 1986 Coretta Scott King.

Langford, Jeremy, *God Moments: Why Faith Really Matters to a New Generation* (Maryknoll, NY: Orbis Books, 2001).

Leddy, Mary Jo, *Radical Gratitude* (Maryknoll, NY: Orbis Books, 2002).

Levertov, Denise, *The Poet in the World* (New York: New Directions Publishing Co., 1973).

Levertov, Denise, *Light Up the Cave* (New York: New Directions Publishing Co., 1981).

Linn, Dennis, Sheila Fabricant Linn, and Matthew Linn, *Don't Forgive Too Soon: Extending the Two Hands That Heal* (Mahwah, NJ: Paulist Press, 1997). Used by permission of Paulist Press.

Main, John, *Essential Writings* (Maryknoll, NY: Orbis Books, 2002). Reprinted by permission of The Continuum International Publishing Group.

Martin, Del, *Battered Wives* (Volcano, CA: Volcano Press, 1970).

Noe, K. Killian, *Finding Our Way Home: Addictions and Divine Love* (Washington, DC: Servant Leadership Press, 2001). © Samaritan Inns, Inc.

Nouwen, Henri J. M., *With Burning Hearts: A Meditation on the Eucharistic Life* (Maryknoll, NY: Orbis Books, 2003).

Nouwen, Henri J. M., *The Inner Voice of Love: A Journey Through Anguish to Freedom* (New York: Doubleday, 1996).

Nouwen, Henri J. M., John Dear, ed., *The Road to Peace: Writings on Peace and Justice* (Maryknoll, NY: Orbis, 2002).

O'Donohue, John, *Anam Cara: A Book of Celtic Wisdom* (New York: HarperCollins, 1997).

O'Murchu, Diarmuid, *Evolutionary Faith: Rediscovering God in Our Great Story* (Maryknoll, NY: Orbis Books, 2002).

Palmer, Parker J., *The Company of Strangers: Christians and the Renewal of America's Public Life* (New York: Crossroad Publishing, 1983).

Phipps, Bill, "Plain-Speaking his Faith," *The United Church Observer* (December 1997).

Quoist, Michel, *Prayers*, trans. Agnes M. Forsyth and Anne Marie de Commaille, (Chicago, IL: Sheed & Ward, 2004).

Ruether, Rosemary Radford, *Gaia and God: An Ecofeminist Theology of Earth Healing* (San Francisco: HarperCollins Publishers, 1994).

Richards, M.C., *Centering: In Pottery, Poetry, and the Person* (New England: Wesleyan University Press, 1989). Reprinted by permission of Wesleyan University Press. All rights reserved.

Rohr, Richard, *Everything Belongs: The Gift of Contemplative Prayer* (New York: Crossroad Publishing Company, 2003).

Snyder, Mary Hembrow, *The Christology of Rosemary Radford Ruether: A Critical Introduction* (Mystic, CT: Twenty-Third Publications, 1988).

Soelle, Dorothee, "How We Speak of God," *The Other Side* (January/February 2001), 10–15.

Spong, John Shelby, *Rescuing the Bible from Fundamentalism: A Bishop Rethinks the Meaning of Scripture* (Scarborough: HarperCollins Publishers Canada, 1992).

Suchocki, Marjorie Hewitt, "Evil, Eschatology, and God: Response to David Griffin," *Process Studies 18, 1* (Spring 1989), 63.

Ware, Corinne, *Connecting to God: Nurturing Spirituality Through Small Groups* (Bethesda, MD: Alban Institute, 1997).

Whitehead, Alfred North, *Process and Reality* (Cambridge: Macmillan, 1929). Copyright renewed © 1957 by Eveylyn Whitehead. Reprinted with permission of Scribner, an imprint of Simon & Schuster Adult Publishing Group.